12

THE LOBSTER KIDS' GUIDE
TO EXPLORING
VANCOUVER

BY JENI WRIGHT

Lobster
Press
Limited

Wright, Jeni, 1951-
The Lobster Kids' Guide to Exploring Vancouver: 12 Months of Fun!
Text copyright © 2000 by Lobster Press Limited
Illustrations copyright © 2000 by Lobster Press Limited

Published by
Lobster Press Limited
1250 René-Lévesque Blvd. West, Suite 2200
Montréal, Québec H3B 4W8
Tel. (514) 989-3121, Fax (514) 989-3168
www.lobsterpress.com

Publisher: Alison Fripp
Editor: Bob Kirner
Senior Editor: Kathy Tompkins
Assistant Editor: Alison Fischer
Production Manager: Allison Larin
Copy Editor and Proofreader: Frances Purslow
Cover and Illustrations: Christine Battuz
Icons: Christiane Beauregard and Josée Masse
Layout and Design: Olivier Lasser

Canadian Cataloguing-in-Publication Data

Biennial.
[2000]-
(The Lobster kids' city explorers series)
"12 months of fun!"
ISSN 1493-7948
ISBN 1-894222-05-9 (2000 issue)

1. Family recreation—British Columbia—Vancouver Metropolitan Area—Guidebooks. 2. Children—Travel—British Columbia—Vancouver Metropolitan Area—Guidebooks. 3. Amusements—British Columbia—Vancouver Metropolitan Area—Guidebooks. 4. Vancouver Metropolitan Area (B.C.)—Guidebooks. I. Title: Lobster Kids' Guide to Exploring Vancouver. II. Series.

FC3847.18.L6   917.11'33044   C00-900421-1

Printed and bound in Canada

*T*his book is dedicated to my late father, Raphael Collins, who inspired me to write.

Undertaking a challenging project such as this one would not have been possible without the help of many people.

I would like to extend a special thanks to my children, Daniel and Ilan, who participated willingly and showed me a child's eye view of Vancouver. I am indebted to my husband and wonderful friend Steve, who provided endless hours of support and assistance, often into the wee hours. And to my big sister Gay, for always believing in me.

I would like to thank my dearest friend, Barb Pesner, who was not only a sounding board for ideas, but was also always available to iron out the computer bugs.

Thank you to Ellen, Heather, Maureen, Janice and Judy, who sustained and supported me through difficult times, and to the Or Shalom community and David Litvak, who brought this project to my attention.

I am especially grateful to my editor, Bob Kirner, for all his encouragement, patience and tireless effort.

Many people went out of their way to help me find information or make arrangements; in particular, Sheliza Mitha at Tourism Vancouver, Cristiana Spooner at the Media Relations Department of Tourism Whistler and Jolie Switzer from the Greater Vancouver Region District.

Finally, I would like to extend my appreciation to Alison Fripp and "the gang" at Lobster Press for all their hard work and for giving me a start in the book business.

I have chosen to donate a percentage of my royalties to "Meow Aid," a Vancouver-based charity that rescues stray cats.

Table of Contents

Author's Introduction

When Alison Fripp approached me to write this book, I was confident that I knew all the best places to take kids in the Greater Vancouver area. After all, I had lived in the city for over 20 years and enjoyed taking my children on outings to parks, museums, festivals and restaurants. Once I began to research Vancouver's attractions, however, I realized that the city had more to offer kids than I had ever imagined.

My family discovered an abundance of inexpensive places around the city that offer kids all kinds of fun and excitement. And you aren't limited to Vancouver's major attractions either. There are also destinations in your neighbourhood that are ideal for family outings. The only problem I encountered while writing this book was figuring out how many of them we could squeeze into each weekend!

So, if you have chosen Vancouver for a family holiday, this guidebook offers lots of ideas to help you become acquainted with the city's kid-friendly places. If you are fortunate enough to *live* here, why not head out and pretend you are tourists in town?

JENI WRIGHT

A Word from the Publisher

L obster Press is proud to present *The Lobster Kids' Guide to Exploring Vancouver*, the next in our series of guidebooks that offer information and ideas for exploring Canadian cities with children. We won't keep you long from enjoying this book, but first we want to highlight a few things so you can get the most out of our guide.

Whether you're a parent, a teacher or a tourist, if you're caring for children between the ages of 1 and 12, this book is ideal for you. It's a complete resource of things to do and see with kids in the Vancouver area, both indoors and out, through all four seasons and for all budgets.

The sites in this guide were visited in 1999-2000 and the information given for each has been verified. However, since prices and opening hours are liable to change and roads are sometimes under construction and some sites close their doors, please accept our apologies in advance for any inconveniences you may encounter.

Take a moment to read about the "Lobster Rating System." It was created to let you know what Jeni Wright and her family thought of each site. Some sites and activities weren't rated because they did not fit all the rating criteria.

Next, familiarize yourself with our icons. We designed them to provide information at a glance and also to give you a smile.

The distances to all the sites and activities were determined from the Hotel Vancouver. We think it is a good meeting point for east, west, north and south.

We welcome your comments. We couldn't include everything that's available for children in Vancouver, so if you feel that we've missed one of your family's favourite destinations, please contact us and we'll print it in the next edition.

A last word: Please be careful when you and your children visit the sites in this guide. Neither Lobster Press nor Jeni Wright can be held responsible for any accidents you or your family might incur.

Enjoy! And watch for the other six books in The Lobster Kids' City Explorers series: The Lobster Kids' Guides to Exploring Montréal, Ottawa-Hull, Toronto, Calgary, Halifax and Québec City.

FROM THE GANG AT LOBSTER PRESS

The Lobster Rating System

We thought it would be helpful if you knew what Jeni Wright and her family thought about the sites in this book before you head off to visit them. Jeni and her two sons rated every attraction and activity they visited for its:

☞ enjoyment level for children
☞ learning opportunities for children
☞ accessibility from the Hotel Vancouver
☞ costs and value for money

A one-lobster rating: Good attraction.

A two-lobster rating: Very good attraction.

A three-lobster rating: Excellent attraction.

Not fitting some of the criteria, and subsequently not rated, are green spaces and various similar, nearby or other attractions.

Table of Icons

These facilities and/or activities are represented by the following icons:

Beach		Parking	
Bicycling		Picnic tables	
Birthday parties		Playground	
Bus stop		Restaurant/ snack bar	
Coat check			
Cross-country skiing		Skating	
		Skytrain station	
Downhill skiing		Snowshoeing	
First aid		Swimming	
Heated chalet		Telephone	
Hiking		Tobogganing	
Ice cream stand		Toilets	
In-line skating		Wheelchair/stroller accessible	
Information centre			
		Wildlife watching	

Getting Ready

Once you've planned an activity for the day, why not take a few minutes and prepare for it. Nothing will ruin an outing faster than forgetting something important at home. These helpful suggestions will ensure your next trip is pleasant for everyone.

☞ Call ahead and verify the site's opening hours and prices.

☞ If you're travelling a considerable distance, pack healthy snacks for everyone.

☞ Remember to bring along liquids.

☞ Pack a road map and a first-aid kit, and be sure that anyone who is taking medication has it with them.

☞ Does anyone get car sick? Bring the Gravol™.

☞ Playing "I Spy," having singsongs and listening to your kids' favourite cassettes while on the road will make the drive more pleasant and delay the inevitable "Are we there yet?"

☞ You already know about packing diapers, wipes and spare clothes. But remember to pack a small toy or two for the baby to play with.

☞ Coloured pencils and scratch pads keep little hands busy on a long drive and while waiting for a restaurant meal.

☞ If you're visiting a park, bring along a Frisbee™, a Hacky Sack™ or a soccer ball.

☞ After a long car ride, take the children to a park before heading to a museum or similar site.

☞ Pack insect repellent, sunscreen, swimsuits, towels and hats if it's summer and you're going to an outdoor site.

☞ Bring extra hats, gloves, scarves, boots and warm coats for outdoor winter activities. Dress in layers, wearing a polycotton or other moisture-releasing fabric next to your body. A dab of Vaseline™ applied to cheeks and noses reduces the risk of frostbite—so can running to the nearest canteen for hot chocolate!

☞ This book uses the metric system where distance is measured in kilometres, height in centimetres, weight in kilograms and area in hectares. Temperature is measured in centigrade. For those unfamiliar with these units:

➤ One kilometre is just over a half mile (0.62 miles).

➤ The minimum height requirement for certain midway rides and waterslides is 122 centimetres (4 feet).

➤ One kilogram is equivalent to a little more than two pounds (2.2 pounds).

➤ One hectare is approximately the same area as two and a half acres (2.47 acres).

➤ Water freezes at 0°C (32°F). When the temperature's 25°C (77°F) it's shorts and T-shirt weather.

Bon voyage!

Getting Around with Young Children

S ome of the sites in this guide are located on expansive grounds and are only accessible on foot. This may be problematic for parents with children in strollers, especially if the walk is over rough terrain. In this guide, sites indicated as being wheelchair accessible are suitable for strollers as well.

TRANSPORTING BABIES

Instead of using a stroller, you might consider carrying your child in a Snugli™. When babies grow out of their Snuglies™ and can hold their heads up properly, they're old enough to be transported in child carrier backpacks. Backpacks are ideal for all types of terrain.

BICYCLING WITH CHILDREN

Today, more and more parents want to include their children on long-distance bicycle rides. If your kids are too young to ride on their own, you can carry them in children's bike seats or in a trailer or trail-a-bike. Used alone or in combination, these accessories provide safe and worry-free bicycling for the entire family. Remember to fit your children with bicycle helmets that have been approved.

CROSS-COUNTRY SKIING WITH SMALL CHILDREN

Even if children lack the technique and stamina to cross-country ski, families can still enjoy a day on the trails using one of two devices for carrying them. A carrier backpack is ideal as long as the adult who is wearing it is a strong skier and avoids steep hills. You can also use a ski trailer. Hiking and bicycle shops carry a variety of makes, but keep your eyes open for quality models such as Scandinavia's Ski-pjulken. Though remember, while the skiers in your party are working up a sweat, any youngster who's in a ski trailer is lying in the cold.

CHAPTER 1

LOCAL ATTRACTIONS

Introduction

Vancouverites are very fortunate to live in a vibrant city that's set amid majestic mountains, the Pacific Ocean and lots of open spaces. Better still, Vancouver and the Lower Mainland are very kid-friendly and have an endless variety of attractions that are fun-filled for families. In the morning, you can head to Grouse Mountain and hike alongside a glacier on a scenic alpine trail and later that same day, take a refreshing dip in the heated, salty waters at Kitsilano Pool. Or visit one of the sandy swimming beaches at Stanley Park where the Children's Farm, the Vancouver Aquarium and other attractions are found.

If the weather turns foul, take the family on an outing that's indoors. Plenty of attractions in Vancouver offer children engaging activities and hands-on exhibits, such as launching a computer-simulated rocket at the H.R. MacMillan Space Centre or crawling through a beaver lodge at Science World. The B.C. Sports Hall of Fame and Museum has all kinds of exhibits for kids to try out. You'll find other local attractions for families in this chapter, including Granville Island, the M.Y. Williams Geological Museum, Vanier Park and the Museum of Anthropology at UBC.

Focus on Fun
SCIENCE WORLD

1455 QUEBEC ST.
VANCOUVER
(604) 443-7443
WWW.SCIENCEWORLD.BC.CA

Housed in what was the Expo Centre during the 1986 World's Fair, Science World boasts fun-filled, interactive displays on subjects ranging from ecology to physics. There's lots to pique any child's curiosity about science be it pedalling a bicycle to generate electricity, solving hands-on puzzles and brainteasers, or walking through a distorted room at the illusions exhibition. Interactive computers located throughout the building entertain and educate visitors about the night sky, the environment and other topics.

If you have young children, take them to the Kidspace Gallery, a spacious play area on the second floor that's filled with construction toys and building blocks. Nearby, the Sara Stern Search Gallery has displays about animals and nature includ-

☞ **SEASONS AND TIMES**
➤ Year-round: Mon—Fri, 10 am—5 pm; weekends and holidays, 10 am—6 pm.

☞ **COST**
➤ Adults $11.75 (with one film $14.75), children (4 to 18) $7.75 (with one film $10.75), under 4 free. Memberships available. All major credit cards accepted.

☞ **GETTING THERE**
➤ By car, take W. Georgia St. east to the Georgia Viaduct and continue east to the Main St. Exit. Go south on Main to Terminal Ave. then turn west to Science World. Pay parking on site. About 20 minutes from the Hotel Vancouver.
➤ By public transit, take city buses 3 or 8 (north on Granville Mall) or 19 (Pender St.), or ride the Skytrain to the Main St. Station. Science World is also accessed via the Aquabus or False Creek Ferries.
➤ By bicycle, use the Seaside Bicycle Route.

☞ **NEARBY**
➤ Chinatown, Dr. Sun Yat-Sen Classical Chinese Gardens, Seaside Bicycle Route.

☞ **COMMENT**
➤ Plan at least a 3-hour visit.

ing a working beehive. Friendly staff regularly give science demonstrations, and 3-D laser shows and OMNIMAX™ films are presented daily (page 131).

Science World has birthday packages (call 443-7505) and offers programs to students (kindergarten to grade 7) that include workshops and tours.

Going for Gold at the B.C. SPORTS HALL OF FAME AND MUSEUM

B.C. PLACE STADIUM
777 PACIFIC BLVD. S.
VANCOUVER
(604) 687-5520

L uring your children away from the Participation Gallery won't be easy. There's so much for them to do, whether it's climbing a rock wall, testing their reactions at the Slap Happy exhibit or sprinting on a 14-metre track against the clock. However, the museum has several other fascinating galleries, such as the Hall of Champions, Builder's Hall and the Discovery and History galleries, where videos, photographs, touch-screen computers and artifacts trace the development of sport in British Columbia.

Most school-age children will want to spend some time at the Terry Fox Gallery viewing memorabilia and watching videos of Terry in the Marathon of Hope, a cross-Canada run he undertook in 1980 to raise awareness for cancer research. At the Rick Hansen Gallery they can learn about another inspiring Canadian who wheeled through 34 countries on four continents to raise money for spinal cord research, rehabilitation and wheelchair sport.

The museum offers educational programs including tours and activities to students of all ages. Birthday parties can be arranged.

☞ **SEASONS AND TIMES**
➤Year-round: Daily, 10 am—5 pm.

☞ **COST**
➤ Adults $6, seniors, youths (6 to 17) and students with ID card $4, under 6 free, families (up to four people) $15.
Group rates available.
Education programs: $3.50 per participant.
Birthday parties: $4 per participant (minimum ten children).

☞ **GETTING THERE**
➤ By car, take Burrard St. south to Robson St., turn east and continue until Beatty St. The museum is just off Beatty inside Gate A at B.C. Place Stadium. Parking lots and meter parking are nearby. Minutes from the Hotel Vancouver.
➤ By public transit, take city bus 5 going east on Robson, or ride the Skytrain to the Stadium Station.
➤ By bicycle or on foot, use the car directions. It's about a ten-minute walk from the Hotel Vancouver.

☞ **NEARBY**
➤Score Virtual Sportsworld, GM Place Stadium, Vancouver Public Library, Chinatown.

☞ **COMMENT**
➤ Plan a 2-hour visit.

Fun for All Seasons
GROUSE MOUNTAIN

6400 NANCY GREENE WAY
NORTH VANCOUVER
(604) 984-0661
WWW.GROUSEMOUNTAIN.COM

Just a short car ride from downtown, Grouse Mountain is a popular destination for skiing, hiking, biking or simply taking in the breathtaking vistas. The Skyride is an aerial tramway that whisks you to the resort on the mountain plateau where a loggers' demonstration, a film, in-season skating, sleigh rides and other activities are included in your ticket.

A network of scenic alpine trails begs to be explored—the Blue Grouse Lake nature walk is the easiest one for children. Afterwards, treat the crew to a meal at one of the resort's restaurants. Weather permitting you can take the chair lift (extra charge) to Grouse's summit and watch hang-gliders lift off. Guided mountain bike tours (recommended for children over 10 with cycling skills) and helicopter tours are offered.

The fun doesn't stop in winter. Grouse Mountain

☞ SEASONS AND TIMES

➤ Year-round: Daily, 9 am—10 pm.
For a schedule of activities,
call 984-0661.
Skyride departs every 15 minutes on the hour.
Helicopter tours: Year-round, call 270-1484 or 1-800-987-4354.
Mountain bike tours: May—Sept, call 924-0288.

☞ COST

➤ Skyride (includes activities):
Adults $16.95, youths (13 to 18) $10.95, children (7 to 12) $5.95, under 7 free, families (two adults, two children) $42.95.
Ski lift tickets (includes the Skyride) start at: Adults $29, youths (13 to 18) $22, children (7 to 12) $16.
Season's passes, special night rates and packages are available. All major credit cards accepted.
Helicopter tours: Start at $50 per person.

THE M.Y. WILLIAMS GEOLOGICAL MUSEUM

25

has over 22 runs for down-hill skiing, some open at night. Instruction is available. There are also snowboarding areas and trails for cross-country skiing and snowshoeing. Equipment for these activities is available at the rental shop. Call 980-9311 for details.

☞ **GETTING THERE**

➤ By car, take Georgia St. west across the Lions Gate Bridge and exit at North Vancouver. At the first set of traffic lights turn north onto Capilano Rd. (it becomes Nancy Greene Way) and follow the posted signs to Grouse Mountain. Free parking on site. About 35 minutes from the Hotel Vancouver.
➤ By public transit, take the Seabus from the terminal at the foot of Granville St. to Lonsdale Quay in North Vancouver. Transfer to city bus 236 at the Lonsdale Quay Bus Loop.

☞ **NEARBY**
➤ Capilano Suspension Bridge, Capilano River Salmon Hatchery, Cleveland Dam.

A Rockhound's Paradise
THE M.Y. WILLIAMS GEOLOGICAL MUSEUM

GEOLOGICAL SCIENCES BUILDING
UNIVERSITY OF BRITISH COLUMBIA
6339 STORES RD.
VANCOUVER
(604) 822-2449

Tucked away in a corner of UBC's sprawling campus, the M.Y. Williams Geological Museum is one of Vancouver's best kept secrets. Named for the distinguished Canadian geologist who headed the university's geology department, the

☞ **SEASONS AND TIMES**
➤ Year-round: Mon—Fri, 8:30 am—4:30 pm.

☞ **COST**
➤ Free (donation requested).

☞ **GETTING THERE**
➤ By car, take Burrard St. south across the Burrard St. Bridge to Cornwall Ave. and go west to Alma St. Turn south to 4th Ave. then west to the UBC campus. Enter at Gate 6 or 7 and park at the West Parkade. It's a short walk uphill from there. About 25 minutes from the Hotel Vancouver.
➤ By public transit, take city buses 4 or 10 south (from W. Georgia St. and Granville St.) to the UBC Bus Loop.

☞ **NEARBY**
➤ Museum of Anthropology, Student Union Building and Aquatic Centre, Nitobe Memorial Gardens.

☞ **COMMENT**
➤ Plan a 1-hour visit.

museum has fascinating displays of crystals, gems, minerals and fossils accompanied by explanatory signs.

Kids will make a bee-line to the huge Lambeo-saurus dinosaur skeleton that's 80 million years old. There are replicas of Mongolian dinosaur eggs on display and the skull and horns of an Irish Elk, the largest deer that ever lived. Many other plant and animal groups are represented in fossils; from algae to corals to fish. The museum's mineral exhibits are just as impressive. You'll see dazzling displays of gold, quartz, amethyst and other glittering gemstones and rarities from all over the world. Guided tours for schools are available.

When younger children start to fidget, take them outside to the courtyard where a pleasant cafeteria serves snacks and refreshments. Or, treat them to a bite and some video games at the Student Union Building that's nearby.

Steering a Course to GRANVILLE ISLAND

BENEATH THE SOUTH END OF THE GRANVILLE ST. BRIDGE
VANCOUVER
(604) 666-5784 (INFORMATION CENTRE)
OR (604) 689-8447 (KIDS ONLY MARKET)
WWW.GRANVILLEISLAND.COM

G ranville Island has something for everyone and lots for kids starting with Adventure Zone, which offers a spiral slide, climbing toys and other enjoyable amusements. A snack bar and arcade are located nearby. Beneath Adventure Zone, the Kids Only Market has shops with goods to satisfy every child's whim, from candy and stuffed animals to clothing and crafts supplies.

Art studios abound on the island and offer everyone the chance to view glass blowers, sculptors and pottery makers at work. And the public market, filled with enticing aromas from exotic and locally grown produce, is a popular spot to shop for seafood, deli items, fresh pasta and cheeses. An island map (available at the Information Centre) will help you find these places and the locations of restaurants, specialty shops, paths, boat rentals, green spaces and toilets. Bring your children's bathing

☞ **SEASONS AND TIMES**

→ Granville Island: Year-round, daily, 9 am—6 pm.
Public Market:
Summer: Victoria Day–Thanksgiving, daily, 9 am—6 pm.
Winter: Thanksgiving—Victoria Day, Tue—Sun, 9 am—6 pm. Closed Christmas Day, Boxing Day and New Year's.
Kids Only Market: Year-round, daily, 10 am—6 pm.
Granville Island Water Park: Victoria Day—Labour Day weekend, daily, 10 am—6 pm.

☞ **COST**

→ Free to browse.
Water park: Free.
Indoor Playground: Tokens can be purchased.

suits and towels in the summer; there's a water park (page 86) that boasts a slide and lots of fun splashy taps and hoses. There are picnic tables, so pick up some goodies at the public market and make a day of your visit.

☞ **GETTING THERE**

➤ By car, take Burrard St. north to Nelson St., turn east to Granville St. and drive south across the Granville St. Bridge. Turn west on 4th Ave. and follow the posted signs for Granville Island. Free and pay parking on site. On summer weekends, look for street parking and walk to the island. About 20 minutes from the Hotel Vancouver.
➤ By public transit, take city bus 50 south on Granville Mall (it stops at the entrance to Granville Island). Or take the Aquabus ferry from the foot of Hornby St.
➤ By bicycle, take the Seaside Bicycle Route.

☞ **NEARBY**

➤ Vanier Park, Maritime Museum, Vancouver Museum, Southam Observatory, Science World, Granville Island Sport Fishing, Model Ships and Model Trains Museum.

☞ **COMMENT**

➤ Plan at least a 3-hour visit.

Go Wild in the City
STANLEY PARK

WESTERN END OF GEORGIA ST.
VANCOUVER
(604) 257-8400
WWW.PARKS.VANCOUVER.BC.CA

Stanley Park is too large to be seen in a single day. So visitors come back again and again to explore its 400 hectares of forests, gardens, beaches, lakes and trails that lead to many kid-friendly attractions. Among them the miniature railway (257-8530), pitch and putt golf (681-8847), the Vancouver Aquarium (page 146), the Children's Farmyard (page 147) and the Lumberman's Arch Water Park (page 87).

To get to these destinations and others within the park you can drive, bike, hike, in-line skate, or go on a horse-drawn wagon tour (681-5115). A free shuttle bus that operates in the summer makes several stops. Among them is Lost Lagoon where the Nature House is located. It's an excellent resource for park visitors and has displays about the local flora and fauna and a reference library. Educational brochures and maps are available and seasonal guided nature walks are offered (257-8544). Or head out for a stroll along the seawall. Its 10 kilometres of paved paths access three supervised swimming beaches and an outdoor pool that's oceanside. Be sure to stop at

☞ **SEASONS AND TIMES**
➤ Stanley Park: Year-round, daily. First, Second and Third beaches: May—Sept, call 738-8535. Second Beach Pool: Call 257-8371.

☞ **COST**
➤ Access to the park: Free (charges may apply for certain activities). First, Second and Third beaches: Free. Second Beach Pool: Call 257-8371.

☞ **GETTING THERE**
➤ By car, take Georgia St. west and follow it to the park. To enter via First Beach, take Burrard St. south to Beach Ave. and go west. Pay parking on site. About ten minutes from the Hotel Vancouver.
➤ By public transit, walk north one block to West Pender St. and turn west to take city bus 135 on West Pender and Thurlow (Monday to Saturday, daytime), or bus 35 (Sundays, evenings and holidays). To access the park's east entrance, take buses 240 or 246. Be sure to ask the driver where to get off.
➤ By bicycle, use the car directions.

☞ **NEARBY**
➤ Lions Gate Bridge.

☞ **COMMENT**
➤ The park's trails are not wheelchair accessible. There's an information centre at the lower parking lot off Pipeline Rd. Plan to visit for the day.

Ceperley Park playground near Second Beach to explore an authentic fire truck.

Concession stands and picnic areas are sprinkled throughout the park and there are restaurants that feature fine dining, such as the Prospect Point Restaurant, which has a children's menu.

Native Lore
THE MUSEUM OF ANTHROPOLOGY

UNIVERSITY OF BRITISH COLUMBIA
6393 N.W. MARINE DR.
VANCOUVER
(604) 822-5087
WWW.MOA.UBC.CA

☞ **SEASONS AND TIMES**
➤ Summer: Victoria Day—Labour Day, daily, 10 am—5 pm.
Other times: Wed—Sun, 11 am—5 pm. Open on Tuesdays until 9 pm. Closed Christmas Day and Boxing Day.

☞ **COST**
➤Adults $6, seniors and students $3.50, children under 6 free, families (two adults and up to four children) $15. Free on Tuesdays after 5 pm.
Annual memberships available. Some credit cards accepted.

This museum's collection of Northwest Coast Native art is among the finest in the world. On display in several galleries are such artifacts as masks, feast dishes, canoes and carvings. The museum has many works by Bill Reid on display, and kids can pat his enormous wooden bear. At the Great Hall you can imagine you're inside a Haida village where magnificent totem poles soar skyward bearing eagles, beavers, ravens, bears and frogs. Elsewhere, you'll find archaeological exhibits, rare European ceramics and a treasure trove of artifacts from around the world, including pottery, baskets and boomerangs.

Most of the museum's exhibits are narrative, which means children younger than eight may be happier exploring the two Haida houses on the grounds outside. Guided tours for school groups (grades 4 and up) are ideal for students studying anthropology and First Nation's sub-

☞ **GETTING THERE**

➜ By car, take Burrard St. south across the Burrard St. Bridge to Cornwall Ave. and go west to Alma St. Turn south to 4th Ave. then go west to the UBC campus. Enter at Gate 6 or 7 and park at the West Parkade. It's a short walk uphill from there. About 25 minutes from the Hotel Vancouver.

➜ By public transit, take city buses 4 or 10 south on Granville Mall to the UBC Bus Loop and walk through the campus.

☞ **NEARBY**

➜ M.Y. Williams Geological Museum, Nitobe Memorial Garden, Student Union Building, Aquatic Centre, UBC Botanical Gardens.

☞ **COMMENT**

➜ There's cafeteria service in the summer. Plan a 2-hour visit.

jects. On Canada Day there's live entertainment with traditional singing and dancing, and children under 12 are admitted free.

Fun in the Sun
KITSILANO POOL AND BEACH PARK

2305 Cornwall Ave.
Vancouver
(604) 731-0011 (pool) or (604) 738-8535

When the weather's fine, head with the gang for a day of swimming at Kitsilano Pool. At 137 metres in length, Kits Pool, as it's affectionately known, is Vancouver's largest outdoor pool with saltwater that's heated. Younger children can frolic safely at the shallow end—the bottom slopes gradually to deeper water—and there are designated lanes for swimming lengths. Lifeguards are on duty and swimming instruction is offered to all levels beginning in early July. Courses in life saving run during May and June. Make sure everyone is wearing sunscreen and a hat, for the pool and pool deck are in full sun. There are change rooms and locker rentals.

There's lots to do out of the pool too. Kitsilano

☞ SEASONS AND TIMES
→ Beach and park: Year-round, daily, dawn—dusk.
Pool: Victoria Day weekend—Labour Day weekend, daily, 9 am—8:45 pm; weekends and holidays, 10 am—8:45 pm.

☞ COST
→ Beach and park: Free.
Pool: Adults $3.80, youths (13 to 18) $2.50, children (6 to 12) $1, families $7.60.

☞ GETTING THERE
→ By car, take Burrard St. south across the Burrard St. Bridge to Cornwall Ave., turn west and continue until Arbutus St. Pay parking on site and street parking. About 15 minutes from the Hotel Vancouver.
→ By public transit, take city buses 2 or 22 south to Kitsilano Beach.
→ By bicycle, use the Seaside Bicycle Route.

Beach Park has a playground, a small water park and picnic tables, some in the shade. Or go beachcombing until showtime at the Kitsilano Showboat (page 132), where live "song and dance" is performed on certain summer evenings.

☞ **NEARBY**
➤ Kitsilano Showboat, Vanier Park, Vancouver Maritime Museum and *St. Roch*, H.R. MacMillan Planetarium, Southam Observatory, Vancouver Museum, Seaside Bicycle Route.

☞ **COMMENT**
➤ Dogs are permitted in the park, but not on the beach.

☞ **SIMILAR ATTRACTIONS**
➤ For listings of pools and swimming beaches around Vancouver, see pages 73 and 104 respectively.

Cosmic Encounters at the
H.R. MACMILLAN SPACE CENTRE

1100 Chestnut St.
Vanier Park
Vancouver
(604) 738-STAR (7827)
www.pacific-space-centre.bc.ca

The Virtual Voyage™ exhibit will be the highlight of your visit at the H.R. MacMillan Space Centre. This cosmic flight simulator takes passengers on a tumultuous voyage of discovery through space. While the ride is not recommended for persons with physical ailments or for the very young, the museum still has lots for them.

The Cosmic Courtyard features interactive exhibits and computer simulations to use for learning about everything from volcanoes to shooting stars. Children can pilot a simulated space shuttle, morph themselves into an alien and touch a real moon rock. There are also displays of space suits and an authentic Apollo moon buggy. A mock-up of the International Space Station can be explored.

At GroundStation Canada Theatre, you'll find interactive multi-media presentations that show how astronauts live in space. Or head to the H.R. MacMillan Planetarium Theatre, where a Laser Light show and astronomy programs are included with the daytime admission.

☞ **SEASONS AND TIMES**

➤ Summer: July 1—Labour Day weekend, daily, 10 am—5 pm.
Winter: Sept—June 30, Tue—Sun, 10 am—5 pm. Closed Christmas Day.

☞ **COST**

➤ Adults (19 to 64) $12.50, seniors, students and youths $9.50, children (5 to 10) $8.50, under 5 free ($5 with Virtual Voyage™), families (two adults and three children) $40.
Group rates and memberships available. Some credit cards accepted.

☞ **GETTING THERE**

➤ By car, take Burrard St. south across the Burrard St. Bridge to Cornwall Ave., turn north on Chestnut St. (it's the first exit off Cornwall) and continue on to the museum. Free parking on site. About ten minutes from the Hotel Vancouver.

➤ By public transit, take city buses 2 or 22 south on Burrard St. to the corner of Cornwall and Chestnut then walk north for a few minutes.
➤ By bike or on foot, use the Seaside Bicycle Route.

☞ **NEARBY**

➤ Vancouver Museum, City of Vancouver Archives, Vanier Park, Vancouver Maritime Museum, H.R. MacMillan Planetarium, Southam Observatory, Kitsilano Beach Park, Seaside Bicycle Route.

☞ **COMMENT**

➤Plan at least a 2-hour visit.

The Heart of the Action
VANIER PARK

NORTH OF CORNWALL AVE. ON CHESTNUT ST.
VANCOUVER
(604) 257-8400
WWW.PARKS.VANCOUVER.BC.CA

Vanier Park is *the* place to go kite flying in Vancouver. You don't have to own a kite to enjoy the spectacle; seeing enthusiasts maneuver their kites to perform aerial acrobatics is worth the visit. Do keep in mind the steady ocean breeze that keeps the kites aloft above English Bay is cooling, so pack extra clothes for everyone.

That done, go exploring the rest of the park and discover its other attractions. There is a beach with clean sand that the kids can play in, however it's unsupervised and the water is very cold. The Seaside Bicycle Route, used by joggers, bikers and those simply out for a stroll, runs through the park connecting it to

☞ **SEASONS AND TIMES**
➤ Year-round: Daily, dawn—dusk.

☞ **COST**
➤ Access to the park: Free.

☞ **GETTING THERE**
➤ By car, take Burrard St. south across the Burrard St. Bridge to Cornwall Ave. and go west until Chestnut St. (it's the first exit). Turn north on Chestnut and continue to the park. Free parking on site. About 10 minutes from the Hotel Vancouver.
➤ By public transit, take city buses 2 or 22 south on Burrard St. to the corner of Cornwall and Chestnut then walk north for a few minutes.
➤ By bike or on foot, use the Seaside Bicycle Route.

☞ **NEARBY**
➤ Vancouver Museum, City of Vancouver Archives, H.R. MacMillan Space Centre, Vancouver Maritime Museum, H.R. MacMillan Planetarium, Southam Observatory, Kitsilano Beach Park, Seaside Bicycle Route.

☞ **COMMENT**
➤ Telephones and toilets are located at the Vancouver Museum and Pacific Space Centre.

Granville Island (page 27) and Kitsilano Beach (page 32). The Vancouver Museum (page 40), the Maritime Museum (page 45), the H.R. MacMillan Space Centre (page 33) and the Gordon M. Southam Observatory (page 120) are all located here as well. Vanier Park is the site for annual events that are popular with families, such as the Vancouver International Children's Festival (page 215) and the Bard on the Beach (page 219).

CHAPTER 2

MUSEUMS

Introduction

For a family outing that's educational and loads of fun, go to one of Vancouver's many museums. Most offer a wide variety of sights and activities designed with kids in mind. Your children can learn about Vancouver's local heritage, fishing, farming, mining and more as they experience hands-on exhibits, watch films and participate in interactive activities. Several museums also have workshops, courses and birthday parties for children.

This chapter tells you all you need to know about these kid-friendly museums. Choosing among them won't be easy, so think of your first museum outing as just the beginning . . . and plan for many more down the road.

NOTE

The following museums, which are covered elsewhere in this guide, also welcome children:

B.C. Sports Hall of Fame and Museum (Chapter 1, page 22)

M.Y. Williams Geological Museum (Chapter 1, page 25)

Museum of Anthropology (Chapter 1, page 30)

B.C. Museum Mining (Chapter 9, page 182)

Burnaby Village Museum (Chapter 9, page 184)

West Coast Railway Heritage Park (Chapter 10, page 208)

Canadian Museum of Flight, Langley (Chapters 12, page 230)

Cruising to the
VANCOUVER POLICE
CENTENNIAL MUSEUM

240 E. CORDOVA ST.
VANCOUVER
(604) 665-3346
WWW.CITY.VANCOUVER.BC.CA/POLICE/MUSEUM

A visit to the police museum is just the ticket for anyone who's fascinated by flashing lights and wailing sirens. Kids especially will love investigating the exhibits at this heritage building where displays ranging from handcuffs to counterfeit money depict the history of law enforcement in Vancouver.

Junior detectives can examine unsolved crime scenes, learn how to take fingerprints and check out a large display of confiscated weapons. Although some kids might feel squeamish, others will be interested in visiting the Coroner's Forensic Exhibit, which features a recreated morgue.

The museum has educational programs that offer students hands-on experience in some policing duties. They'll get to

☞ **SEASONS AND TIMES**
→ Year-round: Mon—Fri, 9 am—3 pm; Sat, 10 am—3 pm.

☞ **COST**
→ Free (donations requested). Family memberships available.

☞ **GETTING THERE**
→ By car, take Burrard St. north to Cordova St. Turn east and continue on until you reach the museum. Street parking. About ten minutes from the Hotel Vancouver.
→ By public transit, take city buses 3, 4, 7, 8 or 50 north on Granville Mall, or ride bus 1 north on Burrard St.

☞ **NEARBY**
→ Chinatown, Vancouver First Firehall No. 1, Gastown.

☞ **COMMENT**
→ Plan a 2-hour visit.

analyze clothing fibres, track footprints and learn about other investigative procedures.

Discovering the Past at
THE VANCOUVER MUSEUM

1100 CHESTNUT ST.
VANIER PARK
VANCOUVER
(604) 736-4431
WWW.VANMUSEUM.BC.CA

T he Vancouver Museum, set in beautiful Vanier Park, houses an extensive collection of artifacts, including archaeological items, artwork, clothing and other displays that trace Vancouver from its prehistory to present day. Although the exhibits are mainly narrative, children should still enjoy their visit.

The "Through My Eyes" exhibition features an array of fine carvings, masks and baskets made long ago by skillful Northwest Coast Native artisans. A magnificent whaling canoe, handmade from red cedar, graces the centre of the room. Elsewhere, kids can explore Vancouver's more recent past. The museum has authentic recreations of an Edwardian home,

---

☞ **SEASONS AND TIMES**
➤ Year-round: Daily, 10 am—5 pm (Thu until 9 pm). Closed Christmas Day.

☞ **COST**
➤ Adults $8, youth (5 to 18) $5.50, under 5 free. Credit cards and debit cards accepted. Memberships available.

a berth on a passenger ship and a railway carriage that arrived in Vancouver with the first CPR passenger train in 1887. Explanatory panels tell you about each exhibit.

The museum has temporary displays that rotate throughout the year. Public lectures, workshops and guided tours often accompany them. Also, tours for schools and other groups with reservations are offered.

☞ **GETTING THERE**

➤ By car, take Burrard St. south across the Burrard St. Bridge to Cornwall Ave., turn north on Chestnut St. (it's the first exit off Cornwall) and continue on to the museum. There are signs. Free parking on site. About ten minutes from the Hotel Vancouver.

➤ By public transit, take city buses 2 or 22 south on Burrard to the corner of Cornwall and Chestnut and walk north for a few minutes.

➤ By bicycle, take the Seaside Bicycle Route.

☞ **NEARBY**

➤ H.R. MacMillan Space Centre, Vanier Park, Granville Island, Kitsilano Beach and Pool, Southam Observatory, Seaside Bicycle Route.

☞ **COMMENT**

➤ Plan a 1-hour visit.

❧❧❧

An Old-Time General Store
THE GROCERY HALL OF FAME

6620 No. 6 Rd.
Richmond
(604) 278-0665

I t's easy to imagine you're stepping back to the 1930s at Canada's only grocery store museum. Everything about the place, from the old-fash-

☞ SEASONS AND TIMES
➤ Year-round: All day on Saturdays. Other times by appointment.

☞ COST
➤ Free (donations are accepted).

☞ GETTING THERE
➤ By car, take Granville St. south across the Granville St. Bridge to 16th Ave. and turn east to Oak St. Go south on Oak across the Oak St. Bridge and access Hwy. 99 S. and continue on until the Steveston Hwy. Exit. Go east on Steveston to No. 6 Rd. and turn north to the museum. Free parking on site. About 45 minutes from the Hotel Vancouver.

☞ NEARBY
➤ Richmond Nature Park, Steveston, Gulf of Georgia Cannery, Britannia Heritage Shipyards, London Heritage Farm, Watermania.

☞ COMMENT
➤ Plan a 1-hour visit.

ioned storefront—once a fixture in downtown Vancouver—to the wooden floors and counters with their displays of goods, recalls a time when shopping at the general store was as much an occasion for socializing as it was a daily chore. Bill Spaner, who owns the museum, is happy to show visitors around if they request a tour in advance. There's an extensive collection of grocery store memorabilia for viewing; from stubby Coca-Cola bottles priced at a nickel each (two bits for a six pack) to antique food tins, ketchup bottles, cereal boxes and more.

The museum has a large selection of collectibles and curios. Featured are wooden iceboxes, butcher blocks, cash registers, scales and an antique apple-coring machine that's still operational. It's little wonder why filmmakers frequent the museum in search of props for their movies.

A Visual Delight
THE CANADIAN CRAFT MUSEUM

639 HORNBY ST.
VANCOUVER
(604) 687-8266

The Canadian Craft Museum is the perfect place to bring kids interested in arts and crafts. The museum, the only one in Canada entirely devoted to multi-media crafts, has displays of jewellery, baskets, rugs, pottery, sculptures and other items handmade by artists from Canada and other countries. The exhibits are rotated frequently so call before you go and find out what's currently being shown. When younger children tire of their visit, they can play in the courtyard at Cathedral Place just outside the museum. It's a pleasant, peaceful spot where you can purchase snacks. The courtyard is the scene of lunchtime concerts in summer months. Schedules are posted in the lobby of Cathedral Place.

☞ **SEASONS AND TIMES**
➤ Year-round: Mon—Sat, 10 am—5 pm (Thu till 9 pm); Sun and holidays, noon—5 pm.

☞ **COST**
➤ $4 per person, children 12 and under free.
Free on Thursday evenings (donations are welcome).
All major credit cards accepted.

☞ **GETTING THERE**
➤ The museum is one block east of the Hotel Vancouver on the north side of Hornby St. inside Cathedral Place.

☞ **NEARBY**
➤ Christ Church Cathedral, Robson Square, Pacific Mineral Museum, Gastown. Provincial and Supreme Courts.

☞ **COMMENT**
➤ Plan a 1-hour visit.

Life in the 1800s
NORTH VANCOUVER MUSEUM AND ARCHIVES

209 W. 4TH ST.
NORTH VANCOUVER
(604) 987-5618

☞ **SEASONS AND TIMES**
➤ Year-round: Wed—Sun, noon—5 pm (Thu until 9 pm).

☞ **COST**
➤ Free. There's a fee for the programs.

☞ **GETTING THERE**
➤ By car, take Georgia St. west across the Lions Gate Bridge and exit at North Vancouver. Drive east along Marine Dr., bearing right onto 3rd Ave., and continue east until Chesterfield where you will turn north. Free parking on site. About 30 minutes from the Hotel Vancouver.
➤ By public transit, take the Seabus to Lonsdale Quay in North Vancouver and walk north along Chesterfield. Or, transfer to city bus 239 or 246.

Although small, this museum located in Presentation House has interesting artifacts that depict North Shore history starting in the late 1800s. Permanent exhibits tell the story of early European settlement in the area and how the inhabitants built the region into what is now a booming community. There are displays about logging and shipbuilding and kids can view old machinery, telephone equipment and an antique piano. If you have the time the archives contain a substantial collection of old black-and-white photographs for perusing, which is a pleasant way to pass an hour or so.

The museum has educational programs for children (summer and winter breaks) and offers one-hour historical walking tours (summers only) along the waterfront, starting from the PGE Railway Station. There are facilities for birthday parties.

☞ **NEARBY**
→ Lonsdale Quay Public Market.

☞ **COMMENT**
→ Presentation House also houses an arts centre with a theatre, a recital hall and a photo gallery. Plan a 1-hour visit.

☞ **SIMILAR ATTRACTIONS**
→ **West Vancouver Archives and Museum,** 680 17th St., West Vancouver 925-7295.

Richmond Archives and Museum, 180 - 7770 Minoru Gate, Richmond 231-6457.

Steveston Museum, 3811 Moncton St., Steveston 271-6868.

New Westminster Museum and Archives, 302 Royal Ave., New Westminster 521-7656.

Setting Sail for the VANCOUVER MARITIME MUSEUM

1905 OGDEN AVE.
VANCOUVER
(604) 257-8300
WWW.VMM.BC.CA

There's a sea of enchanting displays to capture every child's imagination at the Maritime Museum, where boats, pirates and fishing are just a few of the things to investigate. Among the museum's permanent exhibits is the famous *St.*

☞ **SEASONS AND TIMES**
➤ Year round: Daily, 10 am—5 pm.
Closed Mondays from Labour Day to
Victoria Day.

☞ **COST**
➤ Adults $15, children (5 to 19) $7.50.
Annual memberships (family of four)
$35. Major credit cards accepted.

☞ **GETTING THERE**
➤ By car, take Burrard St. south
across the Burrard St. Bridge to
Cornwall Ave., turn north on Cypress
St. (it's the second exit off Cornwall)
and continue on to the museum.
There are posted signs. Pay parking
on site. About ten minutes from the
Hotel Vancouver.
➤ By public transit, take city buses 2
or 22 south on Burrard to the corner
of Cornwall and Chestnut and walk
north for a few minutes.
➤ By bicycle, take the Seaside Bicycle
Route.

☞ **NEARBY**
➤ H.R. MacMillan Space Centre,
Vanier Park, Granville Island,
Kitsilano Beach and Pool, Southam
Observatory, Seaside Bicycle Route.

☞ **COMMENT**
➤ Plan a 2-hour visit.

Roch, which in 1944 was
the first ship to traverse
the Northwest Passage. At
Pirate's Cove kids can play
make-believe pirates and
examine pirate weapons
and a treasure chest. The
Maritime Discovery Cen-
tre boasts interactive computers with games about
nautical history, and there
are big yellow drawers
filled with costumes, puppets, books and scuba-
diving equipment just
begging to be opened.

End your day at the
visitor's lab in the Discovery Centre, where model
ships are restored. Or,
head outside to the Heri-
tage Marina where historic
tugs and other vessels are
moored. Usually, a couple
of boats can be boarded for
inspection. The museum
has facilities for children's
birthdays.

Casting a Wide Net
THE SPORT FISHING, MODEL SHIPS AND MODEL TRAINS MUSEUM

1502 DURANLEAU ST.
GRANVILLE ISLAND
VANCOUVER
(604) 683-1939
WWW.SPORTFISHINGMUSEUM.BC.CA

One visit to this gem of a museum will hook your family and they'll want to come back again. On the first floor you'll find a splendid armada of model ships that includes battleships, tugs and sailboats. All are handcrafted and some are operational. The replica of Jules Verne's *Nautilus* is something that would make even Captain Nemo proud. Elsewhere, there are videos about tuna fishing and salmon fishing, as well as fly-tying and model ship-making. There's a large collection of fishing gear

☞ **SEASONS AND TIMES**
➤ Year-round: Daily, 10 am—5:30 pm.

☞ **COST**
➤ Adults $6, children (5 to 12) $3. Annual family memberships available.

☞ **GETTING THERE**
➤ By car, take Burrard St. north to Nelson St. Turn east to Granville St. and drive south and cross the Granville St. Bridge. Turn west on 4th Ave. and follow the posted signs for Granville Island. Free and pay parking on site. On summer weekends, look for street parking and walk to the island. About 20 minutes from the Hotel Vancouver.
➤ By public transit, take city bus 50 south on Granville Mall (it stops at the entrance to Granville Island). Or take the Aquabus ferry from the foot of Hornby St.
➤ By bicycle, take the Seaside Bicycle Route.

☞ **NEARBY**
➤ Granville Island Market, Kids Only Market, Aquabus, Seaside Bicycle Route.

☞ **COMMENT**
➤ Plan a 2-hour visit.

for viewing and everyone can try their hand at catching salmon on the virtual fishing simulator.

For kids, the highlight of their visit will be seeing the model railroad on the second floor. The display is detailed to scale and features approximately 160 metres of track, scenery and operational trains and streetcars. Old Lionel trains, Meccano construction sets and steam trains complete the amazing layout.

A Glimpse of the Past
DELTA MUSEUM AND ARCHIVES

4858 DELTA ST.
DELTA
(604) 946-9322
WWW.CORP.DELTA.BC.CA/P&R/MUSEUM/MUSEUM-HOME.HTM

☞ **SEASONS AND TIMES**
➤ Year-round: Tue—Sat, 10 am—3:30 pm; Sun, 2 pm—4 pm.

☞ **COST**
➤ Free (donation requested).

Once a municipal hall, a court and a jail, this Tudor-style heritage building offers visitors a glimpse of life in the early 1900s. You can explore the house on your own or take a guided tour (reserve ahead). Several rooms have been restored and furnished for the period. On the ground floor you can visit the kitchen, the study, the nursery and den, and there's an early-century street scene to walk through. Upstairs, you'll find an impressive collection of historical artifacts, including fishing equipment, farm equipment, duck decoys, basketry and weaving. Kids can examine displays of prehistoric tools, perforated stones, flints and toggling harpoons, some dating back 8,500 years. A small discovery room has displays about farming and children can watch a video, ponder quizzes or examine animal hides.

The museum has seasonal events and educational programs for children (Saturdays and March break). There are also programs for families that focus on the history and culture of Delta. Call the museum to register.

☞ **GETTING THERE**

➤ By car, take Granville St. south across the Granville St. Bridge to 16th Ave. and turn east to Oak St. Go south on Oak across the Oak St. Bridge and access Hwy. 99 S. and continue until the exit for B.C. Ferries (Hwy. 17). From Hwy. 17, turn west onto Ladner Trunk Rd. and follow it until Delta St. where you will turn north. Free parking on site. About 40 minutes from the Hotel Vancouver.

➤ By public transit, take city bus 601 southbound on Howe St.

☞ **NEARBY**

➤ Reifel Island, Boundary Bay, Ladner Leisure Centre.

☞ **COMMENT**

➤ Plan a 1-hour visit.

☞ **SIMILAR ATTRACTIONS**

➤ **Surrey Museum and Archives,** corner of 176th Ave. and 60th Ave., Surrey (604) 502-6456.

Richmond Museum, 7700 Minoru Gate, Richmond (604) 231-6440.

Roedde House Museum, 1415 Barclay St., Vancouver (604) 684-7040.

Trooping through the FIFTEENTH FIELD ARTILLERY REGIMENT MUSEUM

2025 W. 11TH AVE.
VANCOUVER
(604) 666-4387

Bessborough Armoury, built in 1932 for the 15th Field Brigade, is home to a small but interesting collection of war memorabilia that includes exhibits of field artillery, war uniforms and examples of small arms. There are photographs and historical documents for studying that detail the role the 15th Regiment played in Vancouver's military history. Of particular interest to kids is the museum's large anti-aircraft gun from WW II.

☞ **SEASONS AND TIMES**
➤ Year-round: Tue, 7 pm—9 pm; Wed, 10 am—2 pm; Thu, 7 pm—9:30 pm. Other times by appointment. Groups welcome.

☞ **COST**
➤ Free (donations welcome).

☞ **GETTING THERE**
➤ By car, take Burrard St. south across the Burrard St. Bridge. Continue south on Burrard until 16th Ave. and turn west to Arbutus St. Go north on Arbutus for a few blocks to West 11th Ave. then turn east one block to the museum. Street parking. About 20 minutes from the Hotel Vancouver.
➤ By public transit, take city bus 16 (Arbutus) south from the corner of Georgia St. and Granville St. to Arbutus and 12th and walk one block.

☞ **COMMENT**
➤ Plan a 30-minute visit.

☞ **SIMILAR ATTRACTIONS**
➤ **Museum of the Royal Westminster Regiment,** 530 Queens Ave., New Westminster (604) 526-5116.

Learning about Rocks at the PACIFIC MINERAL MUSEUM

848 W. HASTINGS ST.
VANCOUVER
(604) 689-8700

The Pacific Mineral Museum, a brand new museum that opened its doors in January 2000, has three galleries with displays for rockhounds of every age. You'll find glittering gems, rare stones and minerals as well as meteorites, fossils and dinosaur bones.

The Discovery Gallery features exhibits that will teach kids about the nature of minerals, such as what they're made of and where they come from, and there are examples of everyday uses for them at the Main

☞ **SEASONS AND TIMES**
➤ Year-round: Tue—Fri, 10 am —5 pm; weekends, 10 am —6 pm.

☞ **COST**
➤ Adults $4, children (3 and over) $3, under 3 free.
Annual memberships available.

☞ **GETTING THERE**
➤ By car, take Burrard St. north to Hastings St. and turn east to the museum. Street parking. Minutes from the Hotel Vancouver.
➤ By public transit, take city bus 1 north on Burrard St.
➤ On foot, use the car directions. It's about a ten-minute walk from the Hotel Vancouver.

NEARBY
➤ CN IMAX™ Theatre, Canada Place, Gastown, Canadian Craft Museum, Christ Church Cathedral.

☞ **COMMENT**
➤ Plan a 1-hour visit.

Gallery. The third gallery, which is located in a vault—the museum occupies a heritage bank building—boasts gold, silver and priceless gems as well as coins, stick pins and other artifacts. Explanatory panels will tell you about each of the displays. Although hands-on exhibits are lacking at the museum, children are permitted to touch many of the specimens and there are lots of buttons for pushing and drawers for opening.

School groups (ten or more) can schedule a guided tour with the curator. For information about educational programs and activities that are being planned at the museum, visit its Web site or call the number above.

Other Museums

These Vancouver-area museums have exhibits suitable for families.

Aldergrove Telephone Museum and Community Archives

3190 271 St.,
ALDERGROVE
(604) 857-0555

You'll find antique telephones, switchboards, telegraph equipment and more for viewing.

B.C. Farm Machinery and Agricultural Museum

9131 KING ST.,
FORT LANGLEY
(604) 888-2273

This museum houses a collection of antique farm machinery and steam engines. You can also visit the blacksmith shop and a working sawmill. Seasonal displays.

B.C. Golf Museum and Library

2545 BLANCA ST.,
VANCOUVER
(604) 222-4653

Features displays about the history of golf. There is a putting green.

Canadian Museum of Flight

5333 - 216TH ST. (LANGLEY AIRPORT),
LANGLEY
(604) 532-0035

Indoor and outdoor exhibits about aviation. Airplanes can be inspected.

Chinese Cultural Centre Museum and Archives

555 COLUMBIA ST.,
VANCOUVER
(604) 687-0282

Photographs depicting the history of Chinese people in Canada as well as examples of calligraphy and on-going temporary exhibits.

Langley Centennial Museum and National Exhibition Centre

9135 King St.,
Fort Langley
(604) 888-3922

E xhibits about early pioneers and First Nations' basketry and tools. On-going temporary exhibits as well.

Simon Fraser University Museum of Archaeology and Ethnology

Burnaby Campus,
Burnaby
(604) 291-3325

A rchaeological and ethnological artifacts on display from First Nations' and other cultures.

Museum of the Exotic World

3561 Main St.,
Vancouver
(604) 876-0073

P ictures, memorabilia and carvings to view from around the world.

PGE Railway Station

Foot of Lonsdale St.,
North Vancouver
(604) 987-5618

Port Moody Station Museum

2734 MURRAY ST.,
PORT MOODY
(604) 939-1648

This former Canadian Pacific Railway station has displays of CPR memorabilia that include a ticket office and a sleeping compartment.

Samson V Maritime Museum

810 QUAYSIDE DR.,
NEW WESTMINSTER
(604) 521-7656

This museum, featuring maritime exhibits, is housed in an old, steam-powered paddle-wheeler that's docked adjacent to Westminster Quay Public Market.

White Rock Museum and Archives

14970 MARINE DR.,
WHITE ROCK
(604) 541-2222

Located in an original train station built in 1913 by Great Northern Railway, the museum has ever-changing exhibits about White Rock, trains and pioneers.

CHAPTER 3

IN YOUR NEIGHBOURHOOD

Introduction

Sometimes you don't need to travel far to find attractions and activities to interest kids. Some of the best places to take children are in your own neighbourhood and most are free or cost very little.

This chapter contains a variety of ideas for outings to public markets, painting studios, craft shops and other everyday places, where a little imagination can turn an ordinary trip into a fun-filled adventure. Have you ever thought about taking your kids to visit the Chinatown Nightmarket or to play Glow Bowling? They'll love it. The telephone numbers and addresses of these and other neighbourhood attractions, including pools, rinks, tennis courts and children's libraries, are provided on the following pages. There is also a listing of Vancouver's more popular and inexpensive family restaurants, as well as the names of several children's hair salons.

Places to Paint
YOUR OWN POTTERY

I f your kids need a new medium for expressing their artistic side, take them to a ceramics studio to paint pottery. You can purchase cups, bowls, piggy banks or a variety of ceramic figures with prices starting at around $5 for some of the smaller items. The studio supplies the paints and brushes, and voila! your children will be occupied creatively for an hour or two.

But you'd better put a limit on the number of pieces you're prepared to buy; younger painters tend to finish their masterpieces quickly and want to do more. It can get expensive. The studio will fire the pottery, so you can drop by in a day or two and pick up the finished pieces.

AARON CERAMICS
7520 6TH ST., BURNABY • (604) 522-5355

CRANKPOTS
153 - 555 W. 12TH AVE., VANCOUVER • (604) 871-0302
160 - 8180 NO. 2 RD., RICHMOND • (604) 204-2475
202 - 1184 DENMAN ST., VANCOUVER • (604) 688-8541

FIRE WORKS CERAMIC STUDIO
101 - 22590 DEWDNEY TRUNK RD., MAPLE RIDGE • (604) 463-8175

JUST KILN TIME
3 - 1864 W. 1ST AVE., VANCOUVER • (604) 732-7994

OCEANSIDE CERAMICS
420 E. COLUMBIA ST., NEW WESTMINSTER • (604) 522-4787

PAINTABLE CERAMICS STUDIO
111 DENMAN PLACE MALL, 1030 DENMAN ST., VANCOUVER • (604) 683-8266

PAINT & FIRE CAFÉ
3436 W. BROADWAY, VANCOUVER • (604) 739-8868

PICASSO'S POTTERY BARN
119 NORTH RD., BURNABY • (604) 444-4410

POTS N NOTS
5 - 9371 NO. 5 RD., RICHMOND • (604) 271-3434

STEVENSON CERAMICS
3900 STEVESTON HWY., RICHMOND • (604) 271-0212

CRAFTY PLACES

At Beadworks your children can select from an extensive selection of beads, baubles and other supplies to design their own necklaces, bracelets and earrings. They can assemble their jewelry at home or at one of the worktables in the shop. Staff are on hand to help when needed. For a fee, Beadworks offers workshops in basic jewelry-making, beading for beginners, gecko designs and more. It also hosts birthday parties (in the store or at your home) that include all the accessories.

BEADWORKS
5 - 1666 JOHNSTON (GRANVILLE ISLAND), VANCOUVER • (604) 682-2323
2316 - 2929 BARNET HWY., COQUITLAM • (604) 941-7098
123 CARRIE CATES COURT, NORTH VANCOUVER • (604) 983-2309

Other Places to Make Crafts

Many community centres in the Vancouver area provide children with arts and crafts instruction in sculpture, clay, pottery and painting. You'll also find courses available at the locations below.

ARTS CONNECTION
12191 - 1ST AVE., RICHMOND • (604) 241-0141

ARTS UMBRELLA
1286 CARTWRIGHT ST. (GRANVILLE ISLAND), VANCOUVER • (604) 681-5268

CRAFT 24
3471 MONCTON ST., RICHMOND • (604) 272-3824

IMAGINEER PRODUCTIONS
103 - 12840 16TH AVE., SURREY • (604) 538-0088

LITTLE SUN CHILDREN'S ART STUDIO
300 - 440 HAZELBRIDGE WAY, RICHMOND • (604) 278-5896

PLACE DES ARTS
1120 BRUNETTE AVE., COQUITLAM • (604) 664-1636

SHADBOLT CENTRE FOR THE ARTS
6450 DEER LAKE AVE., BURNABY • (604) 291-6864

YOUNG AT ART
102 - 20091 INDUSTRIAL, LANGLEY • (604) 533-2787

SCRAPBOOK WAREHOUSE
8932 OAK ST., VANCOUVER • (604) 266-4433

C rafts Canada stores carry everything a child needs to make his or her own album. The stores have Birthday Party Workshops for kids nine and up and card-making workshops for children over four.

CRAFTS CANADA
668 SEYMOUR ST., VANCOUVER • (604) 681-1282
BAY 1 - 1301 UNITED BLVD., COQUITLAM • (604) 520-5949
19878 LANGLEY BYPASS, LANGLEY • (604) 532-1983

T hese shops retail all kinds of supplies for arts and crafts projects.

BAZAAR & NOVELTY
215 W. 2ND AVE., VANCOUVER • (604) 873-5241

DOUGLAS TRADING POST LTD.
840 GRANVILLE ST., VANCOUVER • (604) 687-4024

GRAND PRIX HOBBIES & CRAFTS
3038 W. BROADWAY, VANCOUVER • (604) 733-7114

Rainy-Day BOWLING ALLEYS

Bowling is an ideal rainy-day activity for kids and their parents. Children as young as two will enjoy playing, albeit by their own rules. Many alleys around Vancouver have bowling instruction for all ages and some offer children league play with extra activities and prizes for good scores. You might want to start your kids off with 5-pin bowling as the balls are lighter and easier for little hands to grasp. Some bowling centres, such as SilverCity, have lanes for both 5 and 10-pin bowling, making it fun for the whole family. Others offer Glow Bowling where the alley is illuminated with ultraviolet lighting.

 SEASONS AND TIMES
→ Year round: Daily.

 COST
→ One game: $2.50 to $4.85.
Shoe rental: Varies. Starting at $1 per pair.
Birthday packages: Inquire at the alley.

If kids enjoy the sport—a game among four friends lasts about 45 minutes—they might want to celebrate their birthdays at the lanes. Unless indicated otherwise, these alleys offer packages that generally include a cake, goody bags, snacks and unlimited bowling.

BRENTWOOD LANES BOWLING 10-PIN BOWLING CENTRE
5502 LOUGHEED HWY., BURNABY • (604) 299-9381

COQUITLAM/MAILLARDVILLE LANES
(BIRTHDAYS ARE NOT OFFERED)
9331 BRUNETTE AVE., COQUITLAM • (604) 526-7610

GRANDVIEW BOWLING LANES
2195 COMMERCIAL DR., VANCOUVER • (604) 253-2747

LOIS LANE'S BOWLING & BILLIARDS
175 - 23200 GILLEY, RICHMOND • (604) 540-8182

LUCKY STRIKE LANES
(BABYSITTING AVAILABLE DURING MORNING LEAGUES)
1205 - 6TH AVE., NEW WESTMINSTER • (604) 526-6622

MIDDLEGATE LANES
7155 KINGSWAY, BURNABY • (604) 522-3654

MAPLE RIDGE LANES
22730 - 119TH AVE., MAPLE RIDGE • (604) 467-2626

OLD ORCHARD LANES
4429 KINGSWAY, BURNABY • (604) 434-7644

PARK ROYAL BOWLING LANES
(10-PIN ONLY)
1080 PARK ROYAL S., WEST VANCOUVER • (604) 925-0005

SANDCASTLE LANES
1938 - 152 ST., SURREY • (604) 535-2695

VARSITY RIDGE 5-PIN BOWLING CENTRE
2120 W. 15TH AVE., VANCOUVER • (604) 738-5412

ZONE BOWLING
14711 STEVESTON HWY., RICHMOND • (604) 271-2695

Shopping at a PUBLIC MARKET

The next time you need to shop for fruits and veggies, consider buying them at a public market. These open-air emporiums offer children the sights and smells of fresh farm produce amid the hustle and bustle of commercial activity. While the cost of potatoes, cucumbers, strawberries and other fruits grown by farmers in the Fraser Valley generally match supermarket prices, there's no comparing the quality of produce or the atmosphere. In addition to offering a variety of delectables, some markets feature sweet shops while others, like Granville Island, have a decadent fudge counter where the candy is made before your eyes. Often, you'll find artisans and crafts-makers selling their wares at public markets and buskers performing for the crowds.

GRANVILLE ISLAND PUBLIC MARKET
1661 DURANLEAU, VANCOUVER • (604) 666-5784

☞ Year-round: Daily, 9 am—6 pm.
☞ Closed Christmas Day and New Year's.

LONSDALE QUAY MARKET
123 CARRIE CATES COURT, NORTH VANCOUVER • (604) 985-6261

☞ Year-round: Daily, 9:30 am—6:30 pm.
☞ Closed Christmas Day and New Year's.

NEW WESTMINSTER QUAY MARKET
810 QUAYSIDE DR. (AT THE FOOT OF 8TH ST.), NEW WESTMINSTER
(604) 520-3881

☞ Year round: Daily, 9:30 am—6:30 pm.
☞ Closed Christmas Day and New Year's.

WEST END FARMERS MARKET
LORD ROBERTS SCHOOL, CORNER OF BIDWELL AND PENDRELL ST.
(604) 879-FARM

☞ June—Thanksgiving, Sat, 9 am—2 pm.

EAST VANCOUVER FARMERS MARKET
E. 15TH ST. AND VICTORIA (TROUT LAKE COMMUNITY CENTRE)
(604) 879-FARM

☞ Mid-May—Thanksgiving, 9 am—2 pm (subject to change).

SURREY FARMERS MARKET
10275 - 135TH ST., (NORTH SURREY RECREATION CENTRE)
(604) 591-4576

☞   Late May—early Oct, Sat, 9 am—2 pm.

COQUITLAM FARMERS MARKET
625 POIRIER ST. (COQUITLAM RECREATION CENTRE) • (604) 461-5387

☞   Mid-June—Thanksgiving, Sun, 9:30 am—1:30 pm.

WHITE ROCK FARMERS MARKET
15150 RUSSELL AVE. • (604) 541-2155

☞   Mid-June—mid-Oct, Sun, 9 am—1 pm.

CHINATOWN NIGHT MARKET
PENDER ST. AND KEEFER (BETWEEN MAIN AND GORE)

T he best time to visit Chinatown, with its extraor-
dinary medicine shops, food stores and bakeries,
is in the evening when the Night Market is open.
You'll find everything from exotic fruits to life-size
stuffed animals at affordable prices. Try the dragon's
beard candy made on-site, or sample Bubble tea, an
exotic drink that comes in a variety of flavours.

☞   Chinatown: Year-round, daily.
The Night Market: Mid-May—Sept, Fri—Sun, 6:30 pm—
11:30 pm (weather permitting).

Dining Out at KID-FRIENDLY RESTAURANTS

D ining out with the family offers two rewards: it's fun and it gives the cook in the household a well-deserved break. But if you have many mouths to feed, it can be expensive. Fortunately, there's no shortage of family restaurants in the Vancouver area where diners can choose from a variety of dishes and expect good value. Better still, these establishments are happy to see kids. Many have children's menus and serve kiddie-size portions. Others provide crayons or offer activities to keep the little ones happy. But before heading out with the troops, call ahead to ask if the restaurant has highchairs or booster seats.

CACTUS CLUB CAFÉ
(MILKSHAKES; STEAKS; KIDS' MENU)
1598 PEMBERTON AVE., NORTH VANCOUVER • (604) 986-5776
4653 KINGSWAY, BURNABY • (604) 431-8448
1136 ROBSON ST., VANCOUVER • (604) 687-3278
1530 W. BROADWAY, VANCOUVER • (604) 733-0434

CHIANTI CAFÉ & RESTAURANT
(ITALIAN FOOD; KIDS' MENU; CRAYONS)
1850 W. 4TH AVE., VANCOUVER • (604) 738-8411

HARD ROCK CAFÉ
(TERRIFIC MILKSHAKES; AWESOME DESSERTS; KIDS' MENU; ACTIVITY BOOK)
686 W. HASTINGS ST., VANCOUVER • (604) 687-7625

MARK'S FISASCO
(CRAYONS)
2486 BAYSWATER ST., VANCOUVER • (604) 734-1425

ME-M-ED'S
(PIZZA PARLOUR)
7110 HALL AVE., BURNABY • (604) 521-8881

1121 Austin Ave., Coquitlam • (604) 931-2468
2233 McAllister Ave., Coquitlam • (604) 942-1200

Mr. Mike's Family Steakhouse
(kids' menu)
921 Granville St., Vancouver • (604) 685-5531

Nat's New York Pizzaria
2484 W. Broadway, Vancouver • (604) 737-0707

Rainforest Café
(kids' menu; friendly service; reasonable prices; set in a recreated jungle)
14E 4700 Kingsway, Burnaby • (604) 433-3383

Red Robin Restaurants
(hearty food and decadent desserts; kids' menu; birthday parties; crayons and puzzles; bottomless fries and drinks)
200 - 1001 W. Broadway, Vancouver • (604) 733-6494
801 Marine Dr., North Vancouver • (604) 984-4464
3000 Lougheed Hwy., Coquitlam • (604) 941-8650
10237 - 152nd St., Surrey • (604) 930-2415
7488 King George Hwy., Surrey • (604) 594-6637
9628 Cameron St., Burnaby • (604) 421-7266
22701 Lougheed Hwy., Maple Ridge • (604) 467-6266
112 - 4640 Kingsway, Burnaby • (604) 439-7696

Ricky's Family Restaurant
(Canadian fare; kids' menu)
165 M - 4820 Kingsway, Burnaby • (604) 451-3400
104 - 111 Dunsmuir St., Vancouver • (604) 602-9233
3434 Lougheed Hwy., Vancouver • (604) 253-2027

Romano's Macaroni Grill
1523 Davie St., Vancouver • (604) 689-4334

Shabusen Yakiniku House Ltd.
(If money is no object and you feel like celebrating, try this unique Japanese restaurant where you barbecue your food at the table.)
2993 Granville St., Vancouver • (604) 737-6888

Sodas Diner
(burgers and shakes in a 1950s atmosphere)
4497 Dunbar St., Vancouver • (604) 222-9922
375 Water St., Vancouver • (604) 683-7632

Solly's Bagelry
189 E. 28th Ave., Vancouver • (604) 872-1821
2873 W. Broadway, Vancouver • (604) 738-2570

Sophie's Cosmic Café
(kids' menu, hearty food; 1950s décor)
2095 W. 4th Ave., Vancouver • (604) 732-6810

THE RED ONION RESTAURANT
(GREAT SELECTION OF HOT DOGS AND BURGERS)
2028 W. 41ST AVE., VANCOUVER (604) 263-0833

THE OLD SPAGHETTI FACTORY
(DELICIOUS FOOD; BIG PORTIONS; PLACE MATS FOR COLOURING; COMPLIMENTARY SPUMONI
ICE CREAM; RESERVATIONS RECOMMENDED)
53 WATER ST., VANCOUVER • (604) 684-1288
4154 VILLAGE GREEN, WHISTLER • (604) 938-1081
50 - 8TH ST., NEW WESTMINSTER • (604) 524-9788

THE NAAM
(VEGETARIAN)
2724 W. 4TH AVE., VANCOUVER • (604) 738-7151

TSOLIOS TAVERNA
(GREEK FOOD AND ATMOSPHERE)
2217 E. HASTINGS ST., VANCOUVER • (604) 251-6010

B uffets are fun as kids can select their own dishes, and there's no waiting to be served.

WOODLANDS NATURAL FOOD RESTAURANT
2582 W. BROADWAY, VANCOUVER • (604) 733-5411

ALL INDIA SWEETS & RESTAURANT
6507 MAIN ST., VANCOUVER • (604) 327-0891

PACIFIC ROYAL BUFFET
195 W. BROADWAY, VANCOUVER • (604) 879-7337

THE SUB (STUDENT UNION BUILDING)
CAFETERIA AT UBC
(VARIETY OF FOODS; SUPER DESSERT BAR)
6138 STUDENT UNION BLVD., VANCOUVER • (604) 822-3461

And for dessert . . .

AMATO GELATO CAFÉ
88 E. 1ST AVE., VANCOUVER • (604) 879-9011

ART'S ICE CREAM
2407 W. 41ST AVE., VANCOUVER • (604) 261-6012

COWS VANCOUVER
1301 ROBSON ST., VANCOUVER • (604) 682-2622

MIRIAM'S ICE CREAM
105 - 1184 DENMAN ST., VANCOUVER • (604) 683-7624

MUM'S ICE CREAM
855 DENMAN ST., VANCOUVER • (604) 681-1500
2028 VINE ST., VANCOUVER • (604) 738-6867

SUTTON PLACE HOTEL
(CHOCOLATE BUFFET THURSDAY TO SATURDAY; SEATINGS AT 6 PM AND 8:30 PM)
845 BURRARD ST., VANCOUVER • (604) 682-5511

TIA ANA
5752 VICTORIA DR., VANCOUVER • (604) 327-8615

VANCOUVER GELATERIA ITALIA
1033 VENABLES, VANCOUVER • (604) 251-6958

Popular Fast Food Restaurants

These popular fast food restaurants are located throughout the greater Vancouver area. Treat the kids to a night out and take a stroll to the location nearest you!

BURGER KING

DAIRY QUEEN

KENTUCKY FRIED CHICKEN

McDONALD'S

QUIZNOS

SUBWAY

TACO BELL

WENDY'S

WHITE SPOT RESTAURANTS

Combing the Area for
HAIRCUTS FOR KIDS

For some children, having their first haircut can be upsetting. You can ease their fears and dry their tears by taking them to one of these establishments that cater to kids.

AMADEUS FAMILY HAIR SALON, LTD.
20059 DOLLARTON HWY., NORTH VANCOUVER • (604) 929-1000

2 CUTE 4 U CHILDREN'S HAIR CARE
1433 BELLEVUE AVE., WEST VANCOUVER • (604) 926-4345

THE HAIRLOFT
1496 CARTWRIGHT ST., VANCOUVER • (604) 684-6177

KIDZ KUTZ HAIR DESIGN
227 - 123 CARRIE CATES COURT, NORTH VANCOUVER • (604) 988-4127

KID'S KUT LAND
2624B ST. JOHN'S AVE., PORT MOODY • (604) 937-7455

MINGLES FAMILY HAIR CARE
4804 DELTA ST., LADNER • (604) 946-4848

NASH & COM. HAIR DESIGN
1630 W. BROADWAY, VANCOUVER • (604) 734-4414

SPARKY'S KUTZ FOR KIDZ
806 - 5300 NO. 3 RD., RICHMOND • (604) 270-3333

SYLVIA'S FAMILY BARBER SHOP
6506 HASTINGS ST., BURNABY • (604) 291-7959

Local Treasure Chests
CHILDREN'S LIBRARIES

Visit any municipal library in the Greater Vancouver Region and you'll find a children's section. These days they contain more than books and cozy corners. Your kids will also have access to games, toys, music, interactive computers and Internet facilities. Most libraries have family story times, special events and activities for children throughout the year. At Vancouver's 21 public libraries, children are issued their own membership cards and can borrow books, videos, CDs and magazines for up to three weeks. Better still, they won't be charged overdue fines (neither will parents). If the library doesn't have a copy of the book your child wants, make an acquisition request at the main desk or call InterLINK (437-8441) to find out if it's available for loan at another library in the Lower Mainland.

BURNABY

BOB PRITTIE METROTOWN BRANCH
6100 WILLINGDON AVE.
(604) 436-5410

CAMERON BRANCH
9523 CAMERON ST.
(604) 421-5454

KINGSWAY BRANCH
7252 KINGSWAY • (604) 522-3971

MCGILL BRANCH
4595 ALBERT ST. • (604) 299-8955

COQUITLAM

LINCOLN BRANCH
103 - 3020 LINCOLN AVE.
(604) 464-3430

POIRIER BRANCH
575 POIRIER ST. • (604) 931-1293

DELTA

LADNER-DELTA PIONEER BRANCH
4683 - 51 ST., DELTA
(604) 946-6215

SOUTH DELTA BRANCH
1321A 56TH ST., TSAWWASSEN
(604) 943-2271

NEW WESTMINSTER

NEW WESTMINSTER PUBLIC LIBRARY
716 - 6TH AVE. • (604) 521-8874

NORTH DELTA

NORTH DELTA-GEORGE MACKIE BRANCH
8440 - 112 ST., DELTA
(604) 594-8155

NORTH VANCOUVER

NORTH VANCOUVER DISTRICT PUBLIC LIBRARY
1280 EAST 27TH ST.
(604) 990-5800
WWW.NVDPL.NORTH-VAN.BC.CA

NORTH VANCOUVER CITY PUBLIC LIBRARY
121 W. 14TH ST. • (604) 980-0581
MAIN DESK • (604) 980-4424
CHILDREN'S DEPARTMENT

LYNN VALLEY MAIN LIBRARY
1280 E. 27TH ST. • (604) 984-0286
MAIN DESK • (604) 990-5811
CHILDREN'S AND YOUTH DESK

CAPILANO BRANCH
3045 HIGHLAND BLVD.
(604) 987-4471

PARKGATE BRANCH
3675 BANFF COURT • (604) 929-3727

PORT COQUITLAM

TERRY FOX LIBRARY
2470 MARY HILL RD.
(604) 927-7999

PORT MOODY

PORT MOODY PUBLIC LIBRARY
100 NEWPORT DR. • (604) 469-4575

RICHMOND

BRIGHOUSE BRANCH
100 - 77000 MINORU GATE
(604) 231-6401

STEVESTON BRANCH
4111 Moncton St. (604) 274-2012

SURREY
CLOVERDALE BRANCH
5642 - 176 A St. • (604) 576-1384

GUILDFORD BRANCH
15105 - 105th Ave.
(604) 588-5015

NEWTON BRANCH
13795 - 70th Ave. • (604) 596-7401

OCEAN PARK BRANCH
12854 - 17th Ave. (604) 531-5044

PORT KELLS LIBRARY
18885 - 88th Ave. • (604) 882-0733

WHALLEY BRANCH
10347 - 135 St. • (604) 588-5951

VANCOUVER
CENTRAL BRANCH
350 W. Georgia St.
(604) 331-3600 • (604) 331-3660
Children's Department
WWW.VPL.VANCOUVER.BC.CA

BRITTANIA BRANCH
1661 Napier St. • (604) 665-2222

CARNEGIE BRANCH
401 Main St. • (604) 665-3010

CHAMPLAIN HEIGHTS BRANCH
101 - 3200 E. 54th Ave.
(604) 665-3955

COLLINGWOOD BRANCH
2985 Kingsway • (604) 665-3953

DUNBAR BRANCH
4515 Dunbar St. • (604) 665-3968

FIREHALL BRANCH
1455 W. 10th Ave.
(604) 665-3970

FRASERVIEW BRANCH
1950 Argyle Dr. • (604) 665-3957

HASTINGS BRANCH
2674 E. Hastings St. • (604) 665-3959

JOE FORTES BRANCH
870 Denman St. • (604) 665-3972

KENSINGTON BRANCH
3927 Knight St. • (604) 665-3961

KERRISDALE BRANCH
2112 W. 42nd Ave. • (604) 665-3974

KITSILANO BRANCH
2425 MacDonald St.
(604) 665-3976

MARPOLE BRANCH
8386 Granville St. • (604) 665-3978

MOUNT PLEASANT BRANCH
370 E. Broadway • (604) 665-3962

OAKRIDGE BRANCH,
191 Oakridge Centre
(604) 665-3980

RENFREW BRANCH
2969 E. 22nd Ave. • (604) 257-8705

RILEY PARK BRANCH
3981 Main St. • (604) 665-3964

SOUTH HILL BRANCH
6076 Fraser St. • (604) 665-3965

STRATHCONA BRANCH
592 E. Pender St. • (604) 665-3967

WEST POINT GREY BRANCH
4480 W. 10th Ave. • (604) 665-3982

WEST VANCOUVER
WEST VANCOUVER
MEMORIAL LIBRARY
1950 Marine Dr.
(604) 925-7400 • (604) 925-7408
Children's Department

Cool Places to Play
SWIMMING POOLS

F or kids, the best place to spend a hot summer day is at the local pool. Most community pools, indoor and outdoor, have swimming lessons for children of all ages. Other aquatic sports and lifesaving instruction are also frequently available. Many of these pools set aside a few hours each week for free family swimming. Call your local pool for information about its schedule of activities.

BURNABY

(INDOOR; YEAR-ROUND)

BONSOR INDOOR RECREATION POOL
6550 BONSOR AVE. • (604) 439-1860

C.G. BROWN MEMORIAL POOL
3701 KENSINGTON AVE.
(604) 299-9374

EILEEN DAILLY LEISURE POOL
240 WILLINGDON AVE. • (604) 298-7946

COQUITLAM/PORT COQUITLAM

(INDOOR; YEAR-ROUND)

CHIMO POOL
620 POIRIER ST., COQUITLAM
(604) 927-6969 OR (604) 933-6027

CITY CENTRE AQUATIC COMPLEX
1210 PINETREE WAY, COQUITLAM
(604) 927-6969 OR (604) 933-6027

HYDE CREEK CENTRE
1379 LAURIER AVE., PORT COQUITLAM
(604) 927-7946

(OUTDOOR; SEASONAL)

EAGLE RIDGE POOL
1200 LANSDOWNE DR., COQUITLAM
(604) 927-6969

ROCHESTER POOL
1390 ROCHESTER AVE., COQUITLAM
(604) 927-6969

SPANI POOL
655 HILLCREST ST., COQUITLAM
(604) 927-6969

CENTENNIAL OUTDOOR POOL
LOUGHEED HWY. AND SHAUGHNESSY ST.,
PORT COQUITLAM • (604) 927-7946

ROBERT HOPE OUTDOOR POOL
HUMBER CRES. AND LAMPREY DR.,
PORT COQUITLAM • (604) 927-7946

ROCKY POINT POOL
2800 MURRAY ST., PORT MOODY
(604) 461-7131

WESTHILL POOL
203 WESTHILL PL., PORT MOODY
(604) 936-1211

NEW WESTMINSTER
(INDOOR; YEAR-ROUND)
CANADA GAMES POOL
65 E. 6TH AVE. • (604) 526-4281

NORTH VANCOUVER
(INDOOR; YEAR-ROUND)
KAREN MAGNUSSEN RECREATION
CENTRE
2300 KIRKSTONE RD.
(604) 983-6444 OR (604) 987-7529

LONSDALE RECREATION CENTRE
123 E. 23RD ST.
(604) 983-6444 OR (604) 987-7529

RON ANDREW RECREATION CENTRE
931 LYTTON ST.
(604) 983-6444 OR (604) 987-7529

WILLIAM GRIFFIN
851 W. QUEENS RD.
(604) 983-6444 OR (604) 987-7529

RICHMOND
(INDOOR; YEAR-ROUND)
MINORU AQUATIC CENTRE
7560 MINORU GATE • (604) 718-1300

WATERMANIA
14300 ENTERTAINMENT BLVD.
(604) 448-5353

(OUTDOOR; SEASONAL)
SOUTH ARM OUTDOOR POOL
10100 SOUTH ARM PL.
(604) 718-1335

STEVESTON POOL
4151 MONCTON ST. • (604) 718-1335

SURREY
(INDOOR; YEAR-ROUND)
NEWTON WAVE POOL
13730 - 72ND AVE. • (604) 501-5540

NORTH SURREY RECREATION
CENTRE
10275 - 135TH ST. • (604) 502-6300

SOUTH SURREY POOL
14655 - 17TH AVE. • (604) 502-6200

SURREY SPORTS
AND LEISURE COMPLEX
16509 FRASER HWY. • (604) 501-5950

(OUTDOOR; SEASONAL)
BEAR CREEK POOL
13820 - 88TH AVE. • (604) 501-6300

GREENAWAY POOL
17901 - 60TH AVE. • (604) 502-6257

HJORTH ROAD POOL
10277- 148TH ST. • (604) 502-6257

HOLLY POOL
10662 - 148TH ST. • (604) 502-6251

KENNEDY POOL
9058 HOLT RD. • (604) 501-5158

KWANTLEN POOL
13035 - 104TH AVE. • (604) 502-6252

PORT KELLS POOL
19340 - 88TH AVE. (604) 888-8650

SUNNYSIDE POOL
15455 - 26TH AVE. • (604) 888-8650

UNWIN POOL
6845 - 133 ST. • (604) 501-5156

VANCOUVER
(INDOOR; YEAR-ROUND)
BRITTANIA POOL
1661 NAPIER ST. • (604) 253-4391

KENSINGTON POOL
5175 DUMFRIES ST. • (604) 718-6200

KERRISDALE POOL
5851 WEST BLVD. • (604) 257-8105

KILLARNEY POOL
6260 KILLARNEY ST. • (604) 434-9167

LORD BYNG POOL
3990 W. 14TH AVE. • (604) 228-9734

PERCY NORMAN POOL
RILEY PARK COMMUNITY CENTRE
30 E. 30TH AVE. • (604) 257-8680

RENFREW PARK POOL
2929 E. 22ND AVE. • (604) 257-8397

TEMPLETON PARK POOL
700 TEMPLETON DR. • (604) 253-7101

UBC AQUATIC CENTRE
6121 UNIVERSITY BLVD.
(604) 822-4521 OR (604) 822-4522

VANCOUVER AQUATIC CENTRE
1050 BEACH AVE. • (604) 665-3424

(OUTDOOR; SEASONAL)
KITSILANO POOL
CORNWALL AVE. AND YEW ST.
(604) 731-0011

MAPLE GROVE POOL
YEW ST. AND 51ST AVE.
(604) 266-9512

MOUNT PLEASANT POOL
3161 ONTARIO ST. • (604) 713-1895

NEW BRIGHTON POOL
NORTH FOOT OF WINDERMERE ST.
(604) 298-0222

SECOND BEACH POOL
STANLEY PARK • (604) 257-8371

SUNSET POOL
404 E. 51ST AVE. • (604) 718-6513

UBC AQUATIC CENTRE
6121 UNIVERSITY BLVD.
(604) 822-4521 OR (604) 822-4522

WEST VANCOUVER
(INDOOR; SEASONAL)
**WEST VANCOUVER
AQUATIC CENTRE**
776 - 22ND ST. • (604) 925-7210

Cool Places to Play II
INDOOR ICE RINKS

I f you like to strap on skates, you're in luck. There's no shortage of rinks in the Greater Vancouver area. While hockey, figure skating and other organized activities often dominate ice time, arenas usually set aside several hours a week for family skating. All of the facilities listed here are indoor and some offer skateboarding, roller hockey, ball hockey and lacrosse in summer. Call your local rink for information about its schedule of activities.

BURNABY

BURNABY LAKE ARENA
3676 KENSINGTON AVE.
(604) 291-1261

BURNABY 8 RINKS ICE SPORTS CENTRE
6501 SPROTT ST. • (604) 291-0626

KENSINGTON PARK ARENA
CURTIS ST. AND HOLDOM AVE.
(604) 299-8354

COQUITLAM

COQUITLAM SPORTS CENTRE
633 POIRIER ST. (604) 927-6969
(RECORDED INFORMATION) OR
(604) 933-6000

PLANET ICE
2300 ROCKET WAY
(604) 941-9911

DELTA

LADNER LEISURE CENTRE
4600 CLARENCE TAYLOR CRES.
(604) 946-0211

NORTH DELTA RECREATION CENTRE
11415 - 84TH AVE. • (604) 596-1547

SOUTH DELTA RECREATION CENTRE
1720 - 56TH ST., TSAWWASSEN
(604) 943-0267

NEW WESTMINSTER

MOODY PARK ARENA
701 - 8TH AVE. • (604) 525-5301

NORTH VANCOUVER

ICE SPORTS NORTH SHORE
2411 MOUNT SEYMOUR PKWY.
(604) 924-0828

KAREN MAGNUSSEN RECREATION CENTRE
2300 KIRKSTONE RD. • (604) 983-6444
OR (604) 987-7529

LONSDALE RECREATION CENTRE
123 E. 23RD ST. (604) 983-6444 OR
(604) 987-7529

GROUSE MOUNTAIN
(OUTDOOR SKATING)
6400 NANCY GREENE WAY
(604) 984-0661

PORT COQUITLAM

PORT COQUITLAM RECREATION CENTRE ARENA
2150 WILSON AVE. • (604) 927-7933

PORT MOODY

PORT MOODY ARENA
300 Ioco Rd. • (604) 469-4565

RICHMOND

MINORU ARENAS
7551 Minoru Gate • (604) 278-9704

RICHMOND ICE CENTRE
14300 Entertainment Blvd.
(604) 448-5366

SURREY

CLOVERDALE ARENA
6090 - 176th St. • (604) 502-6410

NEWTON ARENA,
7120 - 136B St. • (604) 501-5044

NORTH SURREY RECREATION CENTRE
10275 - 135th St. • (604) 502-6300

SOUTH SURREY ARENA
2199 - 148th St. • (604) 502-6200

VANCOUVER

BRITANNIA SKATING ARENA
1661 Napier St. • (604) 253-4391

KERRISDALE CYCLONE TAYLOR ARENA
5670 East Blvd. • (604) 257-8121

KILLARNEY COMMUNITY CENTRE
6260 Killarney St. • (604) 434-9167

KITSILANO ICE RINK
2690 Larch St. • (604) 257-6983

RILEY PARK ARENA
50 E. 30th Ave. • (604) 257-8545

ROBSON SQUARE
(OUTDOOR SKATING)
800 Robson St. • (604) 482-1800

SUNSET ICE ARENA
390 E. 51st Ave. • (604) 324-4115

TROUT LAKE COMMUNITY CENTRE
3350 Victoria Dr. • (604) 257-6955

WEST END COMMUNITY CENTRE
1750 Haro St. • (604) 257-8339

WEST VANCOUVER

West Vancouver Ice Arena
786 - 22nd St. • (604) 925-7250

Rallying at
TENNIS AND BADMINTON COURTS

Many recreation centres in greater Vancouver have tennis courts open to the public year-round on a first-come, first-served basis at no cost. Play as long as you want unless people are waiting, in which case 30 minutes is the standard time allotted for play. Most courts offer children instruction in tennis and badminton for a fee, although children must be registered beforehand. Badminton B.C. and Tennis B.C. are referral agencies that will help you find courts, summer camps and lessons around the city. Here are a few numbers to get you started.

BADMINTON B.C.
328 - 1367 W. Broadway, Vancouver • (604) 737-3030

TENNIS B.C.
204 - 1367 W. Broadway, Vancouver • (604) 737-3086

BLUE MOUNTAIN RACQUET CLUB
555 Delestre Ave., Coquitlam • (604) 931-3401

TENNIS IN STANLEY PARK
(604) 605-8224

VANCOUVER RACQUET CLUB
(BADMINTON AND SQUASH)
4867 Ontario St., Vancouver • (604) 874-0242

WESTERN INDOOR TENNIS CLUB
4991 5 Rd., Richmond • (604) 273-7366

Family Place
DROP-IN CENTRES

F amily Place Drop-Ins are a godsend for new parents. While moms and dads share war stories about sleepless nights, their children can make new friends and play with the toys on hand. At most of the centres you'll find friendly experienced staff who are eager to offer advice and support. They also have workshops on relevant family topics as well as social events and fundraisers.

BURNABY FAMILY PLACE
410 CLARE AVE., BURNABY • (604) 299-5112

EASTSIDE FAMILY PLACE
1661 NAPIER ST., VANCOUVER • (604) 255-9841

MARPOLE OAKRIDGE FAMILY PLACE
1305 W. 70TH AVE., VANCOUVER • (604) 263-1405

NEW WESTMINSTER FAMILY PLACE
611 AGNES ST., NEW WESTMINSTER • (604) 520-3666

RICHMOND FAMILY PLACE
6560 GILBERT RD., RICHMOND • (604) 278-4336

SOUTH VANCOUVER FAMILY PLACE
2295 E. 61ST AVE., VANCOUVER • (604) 325-5213

SURREY FAMILY PLACE
10256 – 154TH ST., SURREY • (604) 583-3844

TRI-CITY FAMILY PLACE
3435 VICTORIA DR., COQUITLAM • (604) 945-0048

WEST SIDE FAMILY PLACE
2819 W. 11TH AVE., VANCOUVER • (604) 738-2819

Other Places to Visit

Visiting the Neighbourhood Fire Station

Fire stations are a valuable and necessary resource in our neighbourhoods and the firefighters work extremely hard. However, if all is quiet in the neighbourhood, pop in and visit the friendly firefighters, who are usually happy to show you around the station house. Just be prepared to leave immediately should the fire bell ring!

Used Toy Stores

T oy Traders buys and sells all kinds of used toys. With two locations serving the area, here's the perfect alternative to purchasing new, expensive playthings for your kids.

TOY TRADERS
101 - 5560 - 206TH ST., LANGLEY • (604) 532-9516
1650 E. 12TH AVE., VANCOUVER • (604) 708-0322

CHAPTER 4

PLACES TO PLAY

Introduction

I f it were left up to kids they'd play all day long. Fortunately for them, Vancouver is full of parks, amusement centres and other affordable destinations where children's fun is the number-one priority. At Playland, visitors try out the midway rides. At Splashdown Park, thrill-seekers gravitate to the waterslides. Want to try something else? How about indoor rock climbing, skiing or go-carting? This chapter will also lead you to the best swimming beaches and indoor adventure gyms.

For parents looking to do something extra-special for their child's birthday this year, read on to discover which sites accommodate children's parties. Then make your plans. Days of fun await you.

Hooting and Hollering at
SPLASHDOWN PARK

4799 Nu Lelum Way
Tsawwassen
(604) 943-2251

S plashdown Park, less than an hour from the city, has 13 waterslides that will appeal to every member of the family. Tots can play under gentle sprays at Splash Walk while those a little older head to the Kiddie Area where three miniature slides await. Height restrictions apply on the park's larger slides. Children must be at least 122 centimetres to go on the Whipper Snapper, the Black Hole and the Bonsai Blueline. However, when accompanied by a parent they can enjoy Big Jim's River Run, an excursion for one or two on an inner tube.

☞ SEASONS AND TIMES
➤ Victoria Day weekend—Labour Day weekend (weather permitting).
May: Weekends, 11 am—5 pm.
June: Mon—Thu, 10 am—4 pm.
July—Aug: Daily, 10 am—8 pm.

☞ COST
➤ Individuals (11 and up) $18.75, children (4 to 10) $12.95, families (up to four members) $59.95.
Credit cards accepted.

☞ GETTING THERE
➤ By car, take Granville St. south across the Granville St. Bridge to 16th Ave. and turn east to Oak St. Go south on Oak across the Oak St. Bridge and access Hwy. 99 S. and continue until the exit for B.C. Ferries (Hwy. 17). Follow the posted signs for the B.C. Ferry Terminal. Splashdown Park is a few minutes north of the terminal. Free parking on site. About 45 minutes from the Hotel Vancouver.

☞ **NEARBY**
➤ B.C. Ferries.

☞ **COMMENT**
➤Plan a half-day visit.

☞ **SIMILAR ATTRACTIONS**
➤ **Cultus Lake Waterpark Ltd**.
(about two hours east of Vancouver),
4150 Columbia Valley, Cultus Lake
(604) 858-7241.

➤ **Trans Canada Water Slides**
(about two hours east of Vancouver),
53790 Popkum S., Chilliwack
(604) 794-7455.

The slides are super-vised by lifeguards and there are changing rooms with showers and lockers. Splashdown has a video arcade, a snack bar and tables for eating outdoors. So you can pack a picnic or buy your lunch. Bring plenty of sunblock, as the slides are in full sun.

Surf's Up at
WATERMANIA

14300 ENTERTAINMENT BLVD.
RICHMOND
(604) 448-5353

Watermania, an indoor aquatic centre, promises everyone a rollicking fun-filled time. This may not be Hawaii, but the centre's wave pool generates breakers a metre high at the deep end. At the shallow end of the pool there's a water play structure young-sters love, with water hoses, tunnels, water guns and a slide. Inflatable boats,

☞ **SEASONS AND TIMES**
➤Year-round: Mon—Sat, 6 am—
10 pm; Sun, 10 am—10 pm.

☞ **COST**
➤ Adults $4.75, teens (13 to 18)
$3.75, children (2 to 12) $3.25, under
2 free, families (up to five members)
$9.50.

rings and mats are available. The centre also has two thrilling waterslides, a lane pool with diving platforms and a rope swing for older kids and adults.

Swimming instruction is offered. There are change rooms for men, women and families. Watermania also offers whirlpools, a steam room and sauna as well as a swim and fitness shop, sports therapy clinic and weight room. The centre has facilities for children's birthdays and party packages are available.

☞ GETTING THERE
➤ By car, take Granville St. south across the Granville St. Bridge to 16th Ave. and turn east to Oak St. Go south on Oak across the Oak St. Bridge and access Hwy. 99 S and continue until the Steveston Hwy. Exit. Go east on Steveston to Entertainment Blvd. and turn north. Free parking on site. About 45 minutes from the Hotel Vancouver.

➤ By public transit, take city bus 403 on Howe St. one block west of Granville.

☞ NEARBY
➤ Famous Players SilverCity Theatres, Richmond Ice Centre, Zone Bowling, the Basketball Centre. The Grocery Hall of Fame.

☞ COMMENT
➤ Plan a 3-hour visit.

☞ SIMILAR ATTRACTIONS
➤ **Canada Games Pool**, 65 E. 6th Ave., New Westminster (604) 526-4281.

➤ **City Centre Aquatic Complex**, 1210 Pinetree Way, Coquitlam (604) 927-6999.

➤ **Eileen Dailly Leisure Pool and Fitness Centre**, 240 Willingdon Ave., Burnaby (604) 298-7946.

➤ **Karen Magnussen Recreation Centre**, 2300 Kirkstone Rd., North Vancouver (604) 987-7529.

➤ **Ladner Leisure Centre**, 4600 Clarence Taylor Cres., Ladner (604) 946-0211.

➤ **Newton Wave Pool**, 13730 - 72nd Ave., Surrey (604) 501-5540.

Afternoon Delight
GRANVILLE ISLAND
WATER PARK

SUTCLIFFE PARK AT GRANVILLE ISLAND
VANCOUVER
(604) 666-5784

The growing popularity of spray parks in Vancouver is good news for kids who love water. What child can resist frolicking in water sprays, especially if the weather's hot? Granville Island Water Park has a selection of water toys, including fire hydrants, slides, taps and sprays that will keep the little ones amused for hours. There's also a playground nearby. At mealtime, stroll to the public market where you can purchase fixings for a picnic, or order take-out from one of Granville Island's many food stands and take it back to the park. Spread a blanket on the grass or eat at one of the picnic tables. Hats and sunblock are a must as the park is in full sun.

☞ **SEASONS AND TIMES**
➤ Victoria Day weekend—Labour Day weekend: Daily, 9 am—6 pm.

☞ **COST**
➤Free.

☞ **GETTING THERE**
➤ By car, take Burrard St. north to Nelson, turn east to Granville St. and drive south across the Granville St. Bridge. Turn west on 4th Ave. and follow the posted signs for Granville Island. Free and pay parking on site. On summer weekends, look for street parking and walk to the island. About 20 minutes from the Hotel Vancouver.
➤ By public transit, take city bus 50 south on Granville Mall (it stops at the entrance to Granville Island). Or take the Aquabus ferry from the foot of Hornby St.
➤ By bicycle, take the Seaside Bicycle Route.

☞ **NEARBY**
➤ Vanier Park, Maritime Museum, Vancouver Museum, Gordon M. Southam Observatory, Science World.

☞ **COMMENT**
➤ Plan at least a 3-hour visit.

☞ **SIMILAR ATTRACTIONS**
➤ **Chaldecott Spray Park,** West King Edward Ave. and Wallace St., Vancouver (604) 222-6060. July–Aug, daily, 10 am–4 pm.

➤ **Connaught Spray Park (adjacent to the Kitsilano Community Centre),** Larch St. and 12th Ave., Vancouver (604) 257-6976. July–Aug, daily.

➤ **Lumberman's Arch Water Park,** Lumberman's Arch, Stanley Park, Vancouver (604) 257-8333. July–Aug, daily.

Tag! You're Hit!
PLACES TO PLAY
LASER TAG

Anyone with fond memories of playing tag as a youngster will remember the disappointment of games that ended when a player disputed being tagged it. In today's high-tech version there are no close calls. Players use laser guns to "tag" their opponents and score points electronically. Groups of kids (and grown-ups) can play laser tag and its derivations at several establishments around the Lower Mainland. While the facilities may vary between locations, the rules of the game—which usually last 20 or 30 minutes—are essentially the same. Opposing teams try to outscore each other while travelling through hostile territory. Most of these establishments do not recommend Laser Tag for children under five.

PLANET LASER
7391 ELMBRIDGE WAY
RICHMOND
(604) 821-0770

☞ Year-round: Daily, 10:30 am—midnight.

☞ $6.49 per person per game.

PLANET LASER
20104 LOGAN AVE.
LANGLEY
(604) 514-2282

☞ Year-round: Daily, 10:30 am—midnight.

☞ $6.49 per person per game.

PLANET LAZER EXTREME LAZER TAG
108 - 100 BRAID ST.
NEW WESTMINSTER
(604) 525-8255

☞ Year-round: Daily, 10 am—11 pm.

☞ $6.40 per person per game. Tuesdays all games are two for one. Specials available. Reservations required.

LASERDOME
141 W. 16TH ST.
NORTH VANCOUVER
(604) 985-6033

☞ Year-round: Mon—Thu, 2 pm—11 pm; Fri—Sat, 11 am—midnight; Sun, 11 am—9 pm.

☞ Prices start at $4.25 per game. Specials are offered throughout the week. Reservations required.

Be a Pinball Wizard at
SCORE VIRTUAL SPORTSWORLD

770 PACIFIC BLVD.
VANCOUVER
(604) 602-0513
WWW.VIRTUALSPORTSWORLD.COM

T he whole family can challenge their athletic skills or learn new ones playing virtual golf, basketball, archery, hockey or one of the other sports at this hi-tech arcade. In addition to the virtual games, Score Virtual Sportsworld has more than 70 different video games and simulators. Children ages four and up will find a special area with amusements for them. On the second floor, Skyrink is a large arena (ice-free) that can be rented to individuals or teams wishing to play street hockey, roller hockey, basketball or soccer. Equipment is not supplied. Score Virtual Sportsworld has facilities for children's birthday parties and packages are available.

☞ **SEASONS AND TIMES**
➤ Year-round: Mon—Thu, 11 am—11 pm; Fri—Sat, noon—1 am; Sun 11 am—11 pm.

☞ **COST**
➤ Unlimited game play (one hour) $10.
Unlimited game play (all day) $20.
Skyrink, climbing wall and virtual games extra.

☞ **GETTING THERE**
➤ By car, take West Georgia St. east to Cambie St. Turn south and continue until Pacific Blvd. then head west. Pay parking on site. About 10 minutes from the Hotel Vancouver.
➤ By public transit, take the Skytrain from the Burrard St. Station to the Stadium Station. Walk down the stairs to the exit and head south. Score Virtual Sportsworld is in front of GM Place.
➤ By bicycle, take the Seaside Bicycle Route.

☞ **NEARBY**
→ GM Place, B.C. Place Stadium, B.C. Sports Hall of Fame and Museum,
Science World.

☞ **COMMENT**
→Plan a 2-hour visit.

☞ **SIMILAR ATTRACTIONS**
→ **Playdium @ Metropolis,** 5E - 4700 Kingsway, Metrotown, Burnaby
(604) 433-7529.

→ **Johnny Zee's Amusements Inc.,** 218 - 6200 McKay, Burnaby
(604) 433-6472.

→ **Wiz Zone Computers for Kids.** Fun-while-learning computer classes
for tots (three and up), juniors, seniors and adults. Reservations required.
Computer camps for children and educational software for sale in English
and French. 2014A Park Royal S., West Vancouver (604) 925-1440.

Places to Go
INDOOR ROCK CLIMBING

M ost kids have an innate love of climbing.
Why not satisfy their desire to get higher
with a visit to an indoor centre with rock
climbing facilities? You'll find qualified staff ready
to instruct your children in proper climbing techniques on routes that have been designed to accommodate climbers of every ability. Safety equipment
is provided (running shoes are acceptable footwear)
and supervisory personnel are always on hand.
Children as young as five are welcome. Climbing is
an excellent exercise that builds body strength and

the ability to concentrate—so adults should give it a try too! Many climbing centres have birthday packages.

CLIFFHANGER INDOOR ROCK CLIMBING CENTRE
106 W. 1ST AVE.
VANCOUVER
(604) 874-2400

T wo-hour instruction in basic rock-climbing for children seven and up. Sessions must be prebooked. Also, drop-in Kidrock classes for children 14 and under Saturdays between 10 am and noon. $20 per child includes equipment.

☞ Regular hours: Mon—Fri, noon—10:30 pm; weekends, noon—9:30 pm.

THE EDGE CLIMBING CENTRE
2 - 1485 WELCH ST.
NORTH VANCOUVER
(604) 984-9080

T wo-hour instruction in basic rock-climbing for children five and up Saturdays and Sundays between 1 pm and 3 pm, and Mondays, Wednesdays and Fridays between 4 pm and 6 pm. $18.70 per person includes equipment.

☞ Regular hours: Mon—Fri, noon—11 pm; weekends, noon—9 pm.
☞ $18.70 per person includes equipment.

ROCK HOUSE INDOOR CLIMBING CENTRE
520 - 3771 JACOMBS RD.
RICHMOND
(604) 276-0012

☞ Drop-in sessions every weekend between 10 am and noon. $12.50 per child includes equipment.

☞ Regular hours: Mon—Fri, 10 am—10 pm; weekends, 10 am—8 pm.

VERTICAL REALITY CLIMBING GYM LTD.
202 - 7728 - 128TH ST.
SURREY
(604) 594-0664

☞ Drop-ins (parents and children): Tue—Thu, 3:30 pm—5:30 pm; Sat, 10 am—noon, 2 pm—4 pm and 7 pm—9 pm; Sun, 1 pm—3 pm. $14 per person. Shoe rental $5.

☞ Regular hours: Mon—Fri, noon—10 pm; weekends, 10 am—10 pm.

Running Wild in INDOOR GYMS

D o your children have energy to burn? Take them to an indoor adventure gym where slides, climbing nets, tunnels and obstacle courses are made-to-measure for kids. Even though well-trained staff are on hand, children must be accompanied by an adult.

Some facilities provide play programs with social-izing and music. Others offer organized activities such as arts and crafts, excursions and day camps. You'll

find snack bars at a few of the locations and most
rent space for special occasions such as birthday
parties. In addition to the establishments listed
below, many community centres in the Lower
Mainland have drop-in adventure gym programs
for parents and tots for a small fee.

ADVENTURE ZONE
KIDS ONLY MARKET, GRANVILLE ISLAND
VANCOUVER
(604) 608-6699

☞ Year-round: Daily, 10 am—6 pm.

☞ All-day pass: $5.35 per child. Group discounts available.
Ages 3 to 12.

BONKERS INDOOR PLAYGROUNDS INC.
LANSDOWNE PARK SHOPPING CENTRE
322 - 5300 3 RD.
RICHMOND
(604) 278-7529

☞ Mon—Tue, 9:30 am—5:30 pm; Wed—Fri, 9:30 am—9 pm;
Sat, 9:30 am—5:30 pm; Sun, 10 am—5 pm.

☞ Charges according to child's age ($1.99 to $6.37). No age
limit. Adults free.

CRASH CRAWLY'S ADVENTURE
FUN CENTRE AND LASER TAG
1300 WOOLRIDGE ST.
COQUITLAM
(604) 526-1551

☞ Mon—Sat, 10 am—10 pm; Sun, 10 am—6 pm.
Tots (under 4) $5.75, children (4 and over) $8. Teens are admitted after 8 pm.

THE GATOR PIT
PARK ROYAL SHOPPING CENTRE
2003 PARK ROYAL S.
WEST VANCOUVER
(604) 925-0707

☞ Sat—Wed, 9 am—6 pm; Thu—Fri, 9 am—9 pm.

☞ Tots (under 3) $3.20, children (3 to 12) $6.36.

GO BANANAS
19689 WILLOWBROOKE DR.
LANGLEY
(604) 514-7529

☞ Mon—Thu, 10 am—7 pm; Fri—Sat, 10 am—7:30 pm;
Sun, 10 am—6:30 pm.

☞ Tots (under 3) $3.95, children (3 to 12) $5.95.

Gymboree Play Programs are offered at the following locations with on-going and drop-in sessions. Program times vary according to children's ages. $120 for a 12-week session. For information, call 984-2370.

RYERSON MEMORIAL CENTRE
2195 W. 45TH AVE.
VANCOUVER
(604) 984-2370

ST. DAVID UNITED CHURCH
1525 TAYLOR WAY
WEST VANCOUVER
(604) 984-2379

COQUITLAM SQUARE
109 - 2922 GLEN DR.
COQUITLAM
(604) 469-2323

The following centres also have programs for kids, though the types of activities offered, their costs and schedules vary.

PHOENIX GYMNASTICS CLUB
3214 W. 10TH AVE.
VANCOUVER
(604) 737-7693

UNIVERSITY OF BRITISH COLUMBIA
GYMNASTICS PROGRAM
SCHOOL OF KINETICS
(604) 822-0207

CLUB AVIVA
98 BRIGANTINE DR.
COQUITLAM
(604) 526-4464

OMEGA GYMNASTICS
125B GLACIER ST.
COQUITLAM
(604) 464-1555

Family YMCAs of Greater Vancouver, including:

SOUTH SLOPE
282 W. 49TH AVE.
VANCOUVER
(604) 324-2261

NORTH SHORE
595 BURLEY DR.
WEST VANCOUVER
(604) 926-5541

4970 CANADA WAY
BURNABY
(604) 294-9622

20761 FRASER HWY.
LANGLEY
(604) 530-7946

Whooping It Up at PLAYLAND AMUSEMENT PARK

PACIFIC NATIONAL EXHIBITION GROUNDS
E. HASTINGS ST. (EAST OF RENFREW ST.)
VANCOUVER
(604) 255-5161
WWW.PNE.BC.CA

You'll hear the hollers, whoops and screams long before you get to this popular amusement park. A summer destination for local families and visitors alike for over 80 years, Playland has more than 35 midway rides as well as games of chance. While youngsters enjoy the delightful merry-go-round and other kiddie rides, their older siblings will want to take in every heart-stopping twist and turn on the seven-storey wooden roller coaster. Later, everyone can go on the Ferris Wheel, Playland's oldest attraction, for a stunning view of the surroundings. Or hop aboard the Wild Wasserbaun for an exciting plunge down a waterslide.

When little tummies begin to grumble, you'll

☞ **SEASONS AND TIMES**

→ Early April—mid-June: Weekends and holidays, 11 am —7 pm.
Mid-June—mid-Aug: Daily, 11 am—9 pm.
During PNE (mid-Aug—Labour Day): Daily, 10:30 am—midnight.

☞ **COST**

→ General Passport (all day ride): $17.95.
Limited Passport (under 122 cm): $14.95.
Child accompanied by adult $8, children (under 3) and seniors, free.

☞ **GETTING THERE**

→ By car, take Burrard Street north to W. Hastings St. turn east and continue until Renfrew St. Turn north or south on Renfrew to find pay parking. About 15 minutes from the Hotel Vancouver.
→ By public transit, walk east along W. Georgia St. to Granville St. and take city buses 4, 10 or 16 northbound.

find dozens of food stands on the grounds. Buskers and face-painters roam Playland throughout the day, and there are contests and concerts for kids.

> ☞ **COMMENT**
> ➥ Establish a time and place where family members can meet should you become separated. Plan a 4-hour visit.

Weekdays or evenings are a good time for visiting, as the park is usually less crowded then.

Fresh Air and Fun
CYPRESS BOWL

CYPRESS BOWL RD.
CYPRESS PROVINCIAL PARK
WEST VANCOUVER
(604) 926-5612
WWW.CYPRESSBOWL.COM

Opportunities for recreation outdoors abound near Vancouver. Less than an hour away, Cypress Bowl offers families seasonal skiing, snowboarding, snowshoeing, tobogganing or hiking. Located in Cypress Provincial Park, the Bowl boasts two mountains with 23 runs for downhill skiing day and night. There are three major lifts, including a high-speed quad chair. Even expert skiers will find some of the runs challenging, while there

> ☞ **SEASONS AND TIMES**
> ➥ Park: Year-round, days only.
> Skiing: Dec 1—Apr 30, daily, 9 am—11 pm. For snow conditions, call 419-SNOW (7669).
>
> ☞ **COST**
> ➥ Park: Free.
> Downhill skiing: Adults $35, youths $29, children $17. Discounts for night skiing.
> Cross-country skiing: Adults $12, youths $10.50, children $7.50.
> Season's passes and discount ticket books are available.

☞ **GETTING THERE**

➜ By car, take Georgia St. west across the Lions Gate Bridge and exit at West Vancouver. Go west on Marine Dr. to Taylor Way then turn north and access Hwy.1 W. (Upper Levels Hwy.). Take the Cypress Bowl Rd. Exit and follow the posted signs to the centre. Free parking on site. About 45 minutes from the Hotel Vancouver.

➜ By public transit, take West Vancouver Blue buses 250 or 252 on W. Georgia St. to Park Royal Centre and board the Cypress Shuttle Bus (return fare: adults $7, children $5). The shuttle also departs from Lonsdale Quay. Call 926-1105.

☞ **COMMENT**

➜ Plan a 4-hour visit.

☞ **SIMILAR ATTRACTIONS**

➜ **Mount Seymour** (about one hour north of Vancouver). Seymour's gentle slopes are perfect for novice skiers. Warming hut for kids. Terrain park and half pipe for snowboarders. Tobogganing, equipment rentals and a cafeteria. Trails for hiking. 1700 Mount Seymour Rd., North Vancouver (604) 986-2261. www.mountseymour.com

➜ **Grouse Mountain** (page 24).

are plenty of easier trails for novices.

Cypress Bowl also has 16 kilometres of groomed trails for cross-county skiing, a snowboard park, and hills for tobogganing and tubing. Equipment can be rented, and instruction is available for snowboarding, downhill and cross-country skiing. After a day outdoors, head over to the main lodge where there's a cafeteria that serves snacks and meals.

In summer, Cypress Mountain offers several scenic hiking trails ranging from easy ones lasting about 45 minutes to more strenuous routes that take several hours. For information on the trails and for planning your hike, contact British Columbia Parks at 924-2200.

Sing Along with KARAOKE

F or an afternoon or evening of unbridled fun take your whole family to a karaoke bar or restaurant, where everyone can get into the act. Enthusiasm is all that counts. Kids especially seem unconcerned with their stage presence or ability to sing on key. All they want to know is if their favourite songs are available. Cost varies depending on the number of participants and time of day. Here are the names of a few places to get you started.

MIKE FAMILY KARAOKE
210 - 6200 McKay Ave.
Burnaby
(604) 431-9833

CRYSTAL KARAOKE BOX INC.
130 - 8400 Alexandra Rd.
Richmond
(604) 821-0660

DOWNTOWN KARAOKE BOX
1238 Robson St.
Vancouver
(604) 688-0611

Places to Play PITCH-AND-PUTT

T wo hours and a good sense of humour are all it takes to play 18 holes of pitch-and-putt. While the principle is the same as regular golf—sink the ball in the hole using the fewest

☞ **SEASONS AND TIMES**
➤ Generally Mar—Oct, daily, 8 am—dusk. Call ahead for opening hours.

☞ **COST**
➤ Prices vary between courses for 18 holes, though expect to pay around $7.75 for adults and $4.85 for youths (18 and under).
Club rentals extra. Special rates, season's passes and punch cards are available.
Putting greens (summer only): Adults $2.25, youths (18 and under) $1.10.

☞ **COMMENT**
➤ If it's a sunny weekend, go early to avoid the lineups at Stanley Park and Queen Elizabeth Park.

strokes—players in this scaled-down version use only a putter and a driver. Better still, the holes are shorter and there are fewer hazards. It's a great way to introduce young folks to the game and a fun way to spend an afternoon. Courses in the Lower Mainland have their own systems for booking play. Some operate on a first-come, first-served basis, at others you'll need to reserve ahead. Generally, adults must accompany children under 13. However, the game is not recommended for very small children.

QUEEN ELIZABETH PARK
33RD AVE. AND CAMBIE ST.
VANCOUVER
(604) 874-8336

STANLEY PARK
VANCOUVER
(604) 681-8847

CENTRAL PARK
3883 IMPERIAL ST.
BURNABY
(604) 434-2727

KENSINGTON PARK PITCH-AND-PUTT
5889 CURTIS ST.
BURNABY
(604) 291-9525

MURDO FRAZER PITCH-AND-PUTT
2700 PEMBERTON AVE.
NORTH VANCOUVER
(604) 980-8410

AMBLESIDE PITCH-AND-PUTT
13TH ST. AND MARINE DR.
WEST VANCOUVER
(604) 922-3818

RUPERT PARK PITCH-AND-PUTT
1ST AVE. AND RUPERT ST.
VANCOUVER
(604) 257-8364

Throwing it Long
DISC GOLF

BCDSS (BRITISH COLUMBIA DISC SPORTS SOCIETY)
(604) 878-7387 (HOTLINE) OR 1-888-878-7387

D isc golf is an affordable sport that anyone can play. All that's needed is a little patience and a flying disc. The goal of the game is to throw your disc at a target. You can play it in a park, using trees and rocks as targets. Or go to a disc golf course, where metal baskets or posts and tee-off pads for each "hole" are provided. The disc must be thrown from the spot where it landed, but you can take a couple of steps up to that point to wind up for your throw. Kids will like yelling "fore" just like regular golfers do.

You can learn more about the game by calling the BCDSS or browsing its Web site. Why not watch a game or tournament at one of these locations where disc golf and Ultimate Frisbee™ are played.

MUNDY PARK DISC GOLF COURSE
2300 COMO LAKE AVE. (OFF AUSTIN RD.)
COQUITLAM

JERICHO HILL GOLF COURSE
4TH AVE. BESIDE JERICHO HILL CENTRE
VANCOUVER

LITTLE MOUNTAIN DISC GOLF COURSE
CORNER OF ONTARIO ST. AND 35TH AVE.
VANCOUVER

WINSKILL PARK DISC GOLF COURSE
56TH ST. AND 9TH AVE.
TSAWWASSEN

SEMIAHMOO DISC GOLF PARK
CORNER OF 17TH AVE. AND 147TH ST.
SURREY

Take a Break at
MCDONALD'S™
PLAYLANDS

Did you know your kids are welcome at McDonald's™ play areas even if you don't buy a meal from the restaurant? A godsend during bad weather, these indoor parks feature tunnel slides, carousels and rooms filled with plastic balls. Though the layout varies from outlet to outlet, several tables in each restaurant juxtapose the glassed-in area, allowing parents to sip a quiet coffee while watching the kids. Should you decide to purchase food, children can order a kid-size meal that comes with a toy. Disposable bibs and highchairs are available and the placemats can be coloured, so bring crayons. Birthday parties can be arranged.

☞ **SEASONS AND TIMES**
➤ Year-round: Daily, 7 am—10 pm.
(May vary according to restaurant.)

☞ **COST**
➤ Playlands: Free (meals extra).

Burnaby
4410 Still Creek Dr. • (604) 718-1090

Cloverdale
17960 56th Ave. • (604) 575-1690

Coquitlam
1131 Austin Ave. • (604) 937-4190

Delta and Tsawwassen
5776 Ladner Trunk Rd., Delta • (604) 940-3770
1835 56th St., Tsawwassen • (604) 948-3630

Langley
19780 Fraser Hwy. • (604) 514-1820
20394 88th Ave. • (604) 881-6220

Maple Ridge
22780 Lougheed Hwy. • (604) 463-7858

New Westminster
815 McBride Blvd. • (604) 718-1188

Newton
13565 72nd Ave. • (604) 501-7880

North Vancouver
157 Chadwick Court, Lonsdale Quay • (604) 986-6100
1200 Lynn Valley (604) 904-6000

Port Coquitlam
2330 Ottawa St. • (604) 552-6380

Richmond
7120 No. 3 Rd. • (604) 718-1045
8190 Alderbridge Way • (604) 718-1088

Surrey
10250 152nd St. • (604) 587-3380
8586 120th St. • (604) 507-2250
15574 Fraser Hwy. • (604) 507-7900

Vancouver
160 S.W. Marine Dr. • (604) 718-1040
1527 Main St. • (604) 718-1075
3310 W. Broadway • (604) 718-1080
3450 E. Hastings St. • (604) 718-1099
4455 Main St. • (604) 873-5387
3695 Lougheed Hwy. • (604) 718-1050

White Rock
1789 152nd St. • (604) 541-7010

Sandy Swimming
BEACHES

Nothing beats the heat like a swim at the beach. Blessed with kilometres of breathtaking coastline, the Vancouver area has numerous excellent swimming beaches ideal for an outing with the family. At the following sites, the water is usually clean and there's plenty of fine sand for toddlers to dig in. If you're concerned about water quality, check the local newspaper for the current ratings. Unless otherwise indicated, all of the beaches listed here offer supervised swimming, changing facilities and toilets. Concession stands are usually found nearby.

NORTH VANCOUVER
FOR BEACH INFORMATION CALL (604) 983-6444 EXT. 501 (MAY—SEPT).

CATES PARK AND BEACH
DEEP COVE ROAD AND DOLLARTON HWY.

PANORAMA BEACH
END OF GALLANT ST. AT DEEP COVE

WEST VANCOUVER
FOR BEACH INFORMATION CALL (604) 925-7200 (MAY—SEPT).

ALTAMONT BEACH PARK
PARK LANE AND 29TH ST.
NO FACILITIES.

AMBLESIDE BEACH
CORNER OF MARINE DR. AND 13TH ST.

CAULFIELD PARK
CORNER OF MARINE DR. AND PICADILLY

DUNDARAVE BEACH
CORNER OF 25TH ST. AND BELLEVUE AVE.

EAGLE HARBOUR PARK
EAGLE HARBOUR RD. AND SEAVIEW RD.

JOHN LAWSON PARK
CORNER OF 17TH ST. AND ARGYLE AVE.

KEW BEACH
KEW CLIFF RD.

LARSON BAY PARK
GLENEAGLES DR. AND MARINE DR.

SANDY COVE PARK
MARINE DR. (BETWEEN SHARON DR. AND ROSE CRES.)

STEARMAN BEACH
CORNER OF STEARMAN AVE. AT ROSS CRES.
NO FACILITIES.

WEST BAY PARK
CORNER OF MARINE DR. AND MAPLE LANE

WHYTECLIFF PARK
7100 MARINE DR.

VANCOUVER
FOR BEACH INFORMATION, CALL (604) 738-8535 (MAY—SEPT).

ENGLISH BAY BEACH
BEACH AVE. (BETWEEN BUTE ST. AND STANLEY PARK)
NOT RECOMMENDED FOR SWIMMING.

JERICHO PARK AND BEACH
3900 POINT GREY RD.

KITSILANO BEACH, POOL AND PARK
CORNER OF CORNWALL AVE. AND ARBUTUS ST.

LOCARNO BEACH
N.W. MARINE DR. (BETWEEN TRIMBLE ST. AND SASAMAT ST.)

SECOND BEACH AND POOL
STANLEY PARK (SOUTHWEST SIDE)

SPANISH BANKS EAST
N.W. MARINE DR. (ONE BEACH WEST OF LOCARNO BEACH)

SPANISH BANKS WEST
N.W. MARINE DR. (ONE BEACH WEST OF SPANISH BANKS EAST)

SPANISH BANKS EXTENSION
N.W. MARINE DR. (ONE BEACH WEST OF SPANISH BANKS WEST)
NO FACILITIES.

SUNSET BEACH
CORNER OF BEACH AVE. AND BUTE ST.

THIRD BEACH
STANLEY PARK (WEST SIDE)

TROUT LAKE BEACH (FRESHWATER LAKE)
3350 VICTORIA DR.

Other Places to Play

Richmond Go-Kart Track

**6631 SIDAWAY RD.,
RICHMOND
(604) 278-6184**

For a birthday party or family outing that's exciting and different, head to Richmond Go-Kart
Track, where everyone can take a spin on a kilome-
tre-long track in a gas-operated go-cart. The track
is full of winding curves—there are straight-aways
too—and carts with single or double seats are available. Lots of fun guaranteed. Children must be over
10 years old, or meet minimum height require-
ments, to drive a go-cart. Headgear is required and
is supplied by the track.

☞   Early Apr—late Oct, daily, noon—dusk.

☞ $9 per car (12 minutes). Corporate and group rates available.

☞   Take Granville St. south across the Granville St. Bridge to
16th Ave. and turn east to Oak St. Go south on Oak across the Oak
St. Bridge and access Hwy. 99 S. Take the exit for Shell Rd. and go
south to Westminster Hwy. turn east and drive over the Hwy. 99
overpass to Sidaway and turn south.

Baseball Batting Cages

Batting cages are a fun place to while away an hour
or so. Kids and adults can hit softballs or base-
balls from a pitching machine that has adjustable
speeds. Balls, bats and helmets are usually included in
the price.

NORTH SHORE FUN & FITNESS LTD.
THE BATTER'S BOX
1172 W. 14TH AVE.
NORTH VANCOUVER
(604) 983-0909

A t North Shore Fun & Fitness Ltd., licensed child care is available weekdays between 7 am and 6 pm. The centre also offers indoor golf and instruction is available.

☞ Year-round: Mon—Fri, 10 am—9:30 pm; weekends, 10 am—6 pm. Call ahead for reservations.

☞ Batting cages:
Sept 1—Jan 31: $12 per cage per half-hour. $35 per cage per hour (unrestricted number of players).
Feb 1—Aug 31: $20 per cage per half-hour. $35 per cage per hour (unrestricted number of players).
Indoor golf: $20 per half-hour. $35 per hour (unrestricted number of players).
Discounts available.

THE DUGOUT
110 - 7750 128TH ST.
SURREY
(604) 594-8034

☞ Call for opening hours.

☞ Prices start at $20 for 30 minutes. Unlimited number of batters.

Places to Go Skateboarding

T here's no doubt about it, skateboarding is back in fashion. If your children own skateboards, tell them to grab their helmets and knee and elbow pads, then take in some rollicking good fun at a park

with a bowl for skateboarding. At the locations listed below kids can ride their boards out of harm's
way. Some have obstacles and fun boxes.

BURNABY
CONFEDERATION PARK
CORNER OF WILLINGDON AVE. (NORTH OF HASTINGS ST.) AND ALBERT ST.
(604) 294-7450

COQUITLAM
PINNACLE SKATE PARK
633 POIRIER ST.
(604) 933-6061 OR (604) 927-6969 (24 HOURS)
FEE.

DELTA
LADNER SKATEBOARD PARK,
4550 CLARENCE TAYLOR CRES.
(604) 946-02111

LANGLEY
INDUSTRIAL PARK
CORNER OF 203 ST. AND 62ND AVE.
(604) 532-7529

SURREY
ATHLETIC PARK
14601 - 20TH AVE.

VANCOUVER
CHINA CREEK PARK
CORNER OF E. BROADWAY AND CLARK DR.

WEST VANCOUVER
AMBLESIDE PARK
SOUTH OF MARINE DR. AT 13TH ST.

Ikea Canada

3200 SWEDEN WAY
RICHMOND
(604) 273-2051

Ikea has free supervised babysitting for children
of its customers, on a first-come, first-served
basis. While adults check out the store's selection of
merchandise, kids can play in the ballroom or take

in a video at the mini-theatre. No purchase is necessary to enjoy the service, however, parents must remain on the premises and there is a one-hour time limit. Children must be between 93 and 122 centimetres tall and toilet-trained.

☞   Year-round: Mon—Fri, 10 am—9 pm; weekends, 10 am—6 pm. Call for holiday hours.

☞   Free.

☞   **Similar Attraction**
Lonsdale Quay Ball Room, 123 Carrie Cates Court, North Vancouver (604) 985-6261.

CHAPTER 5

PLACES TO LEARN

Introduction

P art of the fun of parenting is satisfying your children's endless curiosity about the world around them. Luckily, there's no shortage of fun sites in the Vancouver area that can help you do just that. This chapter includes locations where kids can learn about forest ecology, attend a court in session, create their own art treasures, talk to real astronomers, visit a post office and see how salmon are reared. Shhh! Just don't tell them these outings are educational.

Making Art at the VANCOUVER ART GALLERY

750 Hornby St.
Vancouver
(604) 662-4700 or (604) 662-4719 (recorded information)
www.vanartgallery.bc.ca

Some galleries make art accessible to children by offering programs and workshops where they can create their own masterpieces. The Vancouver Art Gallery's Super Sundays are a case in point. This popular event features hands-on activities, drop-in art classes, guided tours and demonstrations. The gallery supplies the materials at no charge and friendly staff will demonstrate art-making techniques to children and their families. Reservations are not required, however, the earlier you arrive the more time you'll have to be creative.

Be sure and reserve some time to explore the rest of the gallery. It has a stunning collection of paintings by Emily Carr, the Group of Seven, and

☞ Seasons and Times

➛ Year-round: Daily, Tue—Sun, 10 am—5:30 pm (Thu until 9 pm).
Super Sundays: Third Sunday of every month between noon and 5 pm.

☞ Cost

➛ Mid-Oct—late Apr: Adults $8, students (with valid ID) $4, children (12 and under) free, families $25.
Free on Thursdays after 5 pm.
Late Apr—mid-Oct: Adults $10, students (with valid ID) $6, children (12 and under free), families $30.
Admission includes Super Sundays.
All major credit cards accepted.

☞ Getting There

➛ On foot, walk east along W. Georgia St. for one block to Hornby St. and turn south. Minutes from the Hotel Vancouver.

☞ Nearby

➛ Robson Street, Canadian Craft Museum, Pacific Mineral Museum, Christ Church Cathedral, B.C. Supreme Court.

☞ Comment

➛ Plan a 2-hour visit.

Canadian and European contemporary artists. Many of the permanent exhibits feature fun-while-learning hands-on activities, and there are programs (such as the Open Studio) to help children appreciate the temporary exhibitions. The museum offers guided tours, workshops and lectures to schools, community groups and the public. Call 622-4717.

All Rise
THE B.C. SUPREME COURT

800 SMITHE ST.
VANCOUVER
(604) 660-2847

Vancouver's law courts are open for visits from the public whenever cases are being heard. Watching a trial makes a perfect field trip for students learning about Canada's legal system, and is a natural follow up after a visit to the Vancouver Police Centennial Museum (page 39). A list that's posted inside the Smithe St. entrance will tell you what cases are being tried that day. Or, wander between the courtrooms until you

☞ **SEASONS AND TIMES**
➤ Year-round: Mon—Fri, 9 am—noon and 1 pm—4 pm.

☞ **COST**
➤ Free.

☞ **GETTING THERE**
➤ On foot, walk east along W. Georgia St. for one block to Hornby St., then head south for two blocks to Smithe St. Minutes from the Hotel Vancouver.

find a case that interests you. Keep in mind that not all of the trials will be suitable for kids. Then take a seat in the gallery and watch the proceedings unfold. You might learn a thing or two about local events before they become news. Guided tours are available for school groups. Call 660-2919.

☞ **NEARBY**
➤ Robson Street, Canadian Craft Museum, Pacific Mineral Museum, Christ Church Cathedral, Vancouver Art Gallery.

☞ **COMMENT**
➤ Plan a 2-hour visit.

☞ **SIMILAR ATTRACTIONS**
➤ Any Provincial Court in the Lower Mainland.

Wild about Wildlife
LYNN CANYON PARK
AND ECOLOGY CENTRE

3663 PARK RD.
NORTH VANCOUVER
(604) 981-3103
WWW.DNV.ORG/PARKS/FUNPARKS.HTM

If you're new to Lynn Canyon, drop by the Ecology Centre, which has kid-friendly exhibits about the resident plant and animal life. Kids can play games identifying wildlife sounds and smells, and put on a show at the theatre that has animal puppets. There's also a video library with over 50

☞ **SEASONS AND TIMES**
➤ **Lynn Canyon Park:**
Year-round: Daily, dawn—dusk.
Ecology Centre:
Year-round: Mon—Fri, 10 am—5 pm; weekends (Mar—Sept), 10 am—5 pm, weekends (Oct—Mar), noon—4 pm. Closed Christmas Day, Boxing Day and New Year's.

☞ **COST**
➤ Access to the park: Free.
Ecology Centre: By donation.

☞ **GETTING THERE**

➤ By car, take Burrard St. north to W. Hastings St. Turn east to Nanaimo St. Go north to McGill St. and head east. Cross the 2nd Narrows Bridge. Take Exit 19 to Lynn Valley Rd. and follow the signs to Peters Rd., then turn east and continue to the end. Free parking on site. About 40 minutes from Vancouver.

➤ By public transit, take the Seabus (at the foot of Granville St.) to Lonsdale Quay in North Vancouver. Transfer to city bus 229 and ride it until the intersection of Peters Rd. and Duval Rd. It's a five-minute walk east on Peters Rd. to the park.

☞ **NEARBY**

➤ Lynn Headwaters Park, Mount Seymour Park, Cates Park, Maplewood Children's Farm, Maplewood Conservation Area, Park and Tilford Gardens, Lower Seymour Conservation Reserve.

☞ **COMMENT**

➤ Plan at least a 2-hour visit.

nature titles and facilities for viewing them.

Perhaps you'd prefer exploring outdoors. Guided nature walks are offered, or you can go it alone on one of the park's well-marked trails. An easy one for families leads across the narrow suspension bridge above the Lynn Creek rapids (hold onto your youngsters' hands) and upstream to 30 Foot Pool. If you follow the creek downstream, you'll arrive at the spectacular Twin Falls. This trail is not accessible to strollers. Ask your kids to watch for the animals they learned about at the Ecology Centre, such as the giant banana slug.

The Ecology Centre has nature walks, craft making, programs on animals and more for families throughout the year. To find out what's upcoming or to arrange a group booking, call 981-3103.

☞ **SIMILAR ATTRACTION**

➤ **Lower Seymour Conservation Reserve (LSCR).** Boasting forests, rivers, lakes and marked trails, LSCR has nature programs for schools and community groups (March to December) and lectures, day camps and weekend programs for kids (summer). Biking and in-line skating (weekdays after 5 pm and all weekend), guided tours (Sundays) and fishing. A fish hatchery, a butterfly garden and Seymour Falls Dam are also found here. Watershed 4400 Lillooet Rd., North Vancouver (604) 432-6410.

Lickety-split! Off to the
POST OFFICE

CANADA POST
349 W. GEORGIA ST.
VANCOUVER
(604) 662-1388

I f you've ever wondered what happens to your letters after you drop them into a mailbox, here's your chance to find out. Canada Post offers guided tours of the letter-handling operation at its main branch in Vancouver. The tours, which take between 25 and 40 minutes depending on your kids' level of interest, are not recommended for children under seven. As your guide provides a commentary, kids can follow the journey that hundreds of thousands of letters make each day along the four-kilome-tre-long spill shoot at the sorting station. They can also watch the Post Office's high-speed machinery au-tomatically sort, postmark and route more than eight pieces of mail per second. Reservations are required.

Leave some time dur-ing the visit to take in the stunning philatelic dis-play at the main lobby of the Post Office building.

☞ **SEASONS AND TIMES**
→ Year-round: Days or evenings, by appointment only (call 277-2303).

☞ **COST**
→ Free.

☞ **GETTING THERE**
→ By car, take W. Georgia St. east. The Canada Post building is located between Homer St. and Hamilton St. Pay parking. About ten minutes from the Hotel Vancouver.
→ By bus, take city buses 26 or 240 going east on W. Georgia St., or ride the Skytrain from the Burrard St. Station to the Stadium Station and walk three blocks west on Georgia St.

☞ **NEARBY**
→ Vancouver Public Library, Queen Elizabeth Theatre and Playhouse, GM Place, B.C. Place, B.C. Sports Hall of Fame and Museum.

☞ **COMMENT**
→ Plan a 1-hour visit.

Each year between 25 and 35 new postage stamps are added to the collection.

Fish and Ladders
THE CAPILANO SALMON HATCHERY

CAPILANO RIVER REGIONAL PARK
4500 CAPILANO PARK RD.
NORTH VANCOUVER
(604) 666-1790
WWW-HEB.PAC.DFO-MPO.GC.CA/ENGLISH/FACILITIES/CAPILANO/CAPILANO.HTM

The Capilano Salmon Hatchery, which is dedicated to preserving wild salmon stocks, is the final destination for thousands of coho, chinook and steelhead that migrate to the Capilano River each year and spawn. The hatchery is open to visits from the public year-round, however, summer is the best time to go with kids. That's when staff are usually available to answer questions. During the school year, call to book group tours where kids can learn what happens behind-the-scenes at the hatchery.

From the underwater observation gallery, they'll view adult salmon lunging

☞ **SEASONS AND TIMES**
➔ Year-round: Daily, dawn—dusk.

☞ **COST**
➔ Free.

☞ **GETTING THERE**
➔ By car, take Georgia St. west through Stanley Park. Cross the Lions Gate Bridge and take the exit for North Vancouver. Turn north at the first set of traffic lights onto Capilano Rd., continuing on for approximately five kilometres. Free parking on site. About 15 minutes from the Hotel Vancouver.
➔ By public transit, take the Seabus (at the foot of Granville St.) to Lonsdale Quay in North Vancouver and transfer to bus 236 (Grouse Mountain).

up the fish ladder to a large holding tank and perhaps see workers harvest the females' eggs for fertilization. After the eggs hatch, the young salmon (called fry) are transferred to holding tanks where they are cared for until they're big enough to be released in

☞ **NEARBY**
→ Capilano Suspension Bridge, Grouse Mountain, Cypress Mountain.

☞ **COMMENT**
→ Plan a 2-hour visit.

☞ **SIMILAR ATTRACTIONS**
→ **Tynehead Regional Park and Fish Hatchery,** off 168th St. and 96th Ave., Surrey (604) 432-6350.

the wild. Narrative displays inside the hatchery tell more about salmon and their natural history.

The Cleveland Dam and Capilano Lake are about ten minutes north of the hatchery. The lake, which is actually a reservoir, is Vancouver's main source for drinking water and a beautiful setting for a picnic. Tours of the dam and reservoir are offered Thursdays to Sundays in the summer at no charge (call 432-6430).

Star Struck at the SOUTHAM OBSERVATORY

1100 CHESTNUT ST.
VANIER PARK
VANCOUVER
(604) 738-7827
WWW.PACIFIC-SPACE-CENTRE.BC.CA

O n a clear evening, take the family for some stargazing at the Gordon Southam Observatory. The Observatory has a 500-millimetre telescope that the public is invited to use for viewing Saturn's rings, Jupiter's moons, Venus and other celestial bodies. Volunteer astronomers, both amateur and professional, will explain about what you are seeing and gladly answer any questions you have about astronomy. A different viewing schedule is presented each evening, so call ahead and find out what is showing.

The observatory is a popular destination for area residents and there are often lineups to get in. So bring sweaters for everyone to ward off the nighttime chill. The observatory is also open during the day on some Fridays

---

☞ **SEASONS AND TIMES**
➤ Year round: Fridays and weekends, 7 pm—11 pm. Weather permitting.

☞ **COST**
➤ Free.

☞ **GETTING THERE**
➤ By car, take Burrard St. south across the Burrard St. Bridge to Cornwall Ave. and go west until Cypress St. (it's the second exit). Turn north on Cypress and follow the signs to the Observatory. Free parking on site. About 15 minutes from the Hotel Vancouver.
➤ By public transit, take city buses 2 or 22 south on Burrard to Cornwall and Chestnut, then walk north for a few minutes.
➤ By bicycle, take the Seaside Bicycle Route.

and Saturdays for viewing the sun. However, this is subject to favourable weather and the availability of volunteers.

☞ **NEARBY**
→ H.R. MacMillan Space Centre, Vancouver Museum, Vanier Park, Seaside Bicycle Route, Granville Island, Kitsilano Beach and Pool, Maritime Museum.

☞ **COMMENT**
→ Plan a 1-hour visit.

☞ **SIMILAR ATTRACTION**
→ **UBC Observatory, Geo Physics Astronomy Building,** 2219 Main Mall, Vancouver (604) 822-2267.

An Education in Wetlands
BURNS BOG

BURNS BOG CONSERVATION SOCIETY
KENNEDY HEIGHTS SHOPPING CENTRE (ADMINISTRATION OFFICES)
202 - 11961 88TH AVE.
DELTA
(604) 572-0373
WWW.BURNSBOG.PACONLINE.NET

Wetlands are magical places, and Burns Bog, a unique, untamed ecosystem on the northern edge of the Delta Nature Reserve, is an excellent example. Black bears, coyotes, beavers and reptiles all make their homes here as do at least 150 bird species, including the endangered sandhill crane. You'll also find sundew, a carnivorous plant,

☞ **SEASONS AND TIMES**
→ Year-round: Daily, dawn—dusk.

☞ **COST**
→ Free.

☞ **GETTING THERE**

➤ By car, take Granville St. south across the Granville St. Bridge to 16th Ave. and turn east to Oak St. Go south on Oak across the Oak St. Bridge, access Hwy. 99 S. and continue until Exit 37 (Hwy. 91). Take it east and exit at River Rd. immediately after the Alex Fraser Bridge. Turn east at the second light onto Nordel Ct. and follow it to the end. There's free parking at the Great Pacific Forum Sports Complex. A brick pathway at the eastern edge of the lot will lead you to the Delta Nature Reserve if you follow it north under the Nordel Way overpass. About 45 minutes from the Hotel Vancouver.

and dwarf pines, mosses and ferns.

Several routes access the bog, though the easiest one is from the Delta Nature Reserve entrance where a paved path makes walking easy for children. It will take you about an hour of hiking just to reach the bog, however, so plan on at least a half-day outing. At the bog, be sure everyone follows the trail, for their safety and to protect the fragile ecosystem. There are no interpretive signs, so animal and plant identification guides and binoculars will come in handy. Pack extra clothing and footwear in case what you are wearing gets wet or muddy. Bring liquids, snacks and bug repellent as well.

Keep your eyes peeled during the visit. New plant and animal species are always being discovered at the bog and you could be the next person to spot one! Before you head out, contact the Conservation Society to obtain a map.

Walking the Labyrinth
ST. PAUL'S ANGLICAN CHURCH

1130 JERVIS ST.
VANCOUVER
(604) 685-6832

If you're looking for something different to do with your children, take them for a short visit to St. Paul's Anglican Church where they can walk the paths of the labyrinth. Many European cathedrals and churches built in the 12th century had labyrinths that people could walk while they prayed or meditated, and the one at St. Paul's, which measures almost 14 metres diagonally, is modelled after the labyrinth found at Chartres Cathedral in France. Depending on your pace, it will take between 5 to 20 minutes to follow the path to the centre, although kids will think it's great sport to run through as fast as they can. Just ask them to remove their shoes before they do.

☞ **SEASONS AND TIMES**
➜ Year-round: Mon—Fri, 8:30 am—9:30 am; Sat, 10 am—noon; Sun, 9:30 am—12:30 pm; last Friday of the month, 7 pm—9 pm.

☞ **COST**
➜ Free.

☞ **GETTING THERE**
➜ By car, take Burrard St. south to Davie St., turn west and continue along Davie until Jervis St. Look for parking on Davie. St. as Jervis St. is a no entry. St. Paul's is one block north. About five minutes from the Hotel Vancouver.
➜ By public transit, take city buses 2 or 22 south on Burrard St.

☞ **NEARBY**
➜ Vancouver Art Gallery, Christ Church Cathedral, Provincial and Supreme Courts, Stanley Park.

☞ **COMMENT**
➜ Plan a 30-minute visit.

Other Places to Learn

The B.C. Ambulance Service

(604) 660-6897

I t's not every day that children can examine an ambulance. However, thanks to a program that's sponsored by their local union, Vancouver-area paramedics will bring their rigs to schools, community organizations and daycare centres to show audiences what the inside of an ambulance looks like and explain a bit about their jobs.

After selecting a victim from the group, the paramedics will apply simulated first aid and then transport the patient on a stretcher into the ambulance. Kids get to see the equipment paramedics use for saving lives, including emergency medical supplies, oxygen tanks and more.

The visits must be scheduled ahead of time and are for groups of ten or more.

☞   Year-round. Call the number above to arrange a visit.

☞   Free.

CHAPTER 6

MUSIC, THEATRE
DANCE & CINEMA

Introduction

W hen we think of "culture vultures," we usually think of adults. But take your children to the Vancouver Symphony Orchestra Kids Koncerts or out for an evening of Theatre Under the Stars in Stanley Park and you'll see that the love of the arts has no age limit. Many theatres and cultural centres around town have regular presentations of music, variety, drama and dance that never fail to enchant younger audiences. This chapter contains a rundown of the venues that stage productions appropriate for kids. You'll also find an idea or two for places where children can receive instruction in the performing arts, including music, ballet, acting and clowning lessons. If you enjoy watching quality movies, we've provided the names of a film festival and repertory movie houses offering cinema for kids or families.

It's Showtime at the VANCOUVER EAST CULTURAL CENTRE

1895 E. VENABLES ST.
VANCOUVER
(604) 254-9578 OR (604) 280-4444 (TICKETMASTER)

Some of the finest children's performers around are featured at the very popular Saturday afternoon Kids Series. See local talent as well as touring entertainers put on puppet shows, perform mime, drumming and plays for kids of all ages. There are six concerts in the series, and the shows usually last one hour. Tickets sell out quickly, so be sure to reserve yours early. Call the centre for a schedule of its upcoming performances.

☞ **SEASONS AND TIMES**
➤ Sept—May: Select Saturdays, 2 pm.

☞ **COST**
➤ $18 for four people.

☞ **GETTING THERE**
➤ By car, take W. Georgia St. east (its name changes to E. Georgia) and drive over the E. Georgia Viaduct. Its name changes to first Prior St. and then Venables St., but continue going east until Victoria Dr. Limited free parking on site. About 30 minutes from the Hotel Vancouver.
➤ By public transit, take city bus 20 from Granville St. and get off at Commercial Dr. and Venables St.

The Play's the Thing THEATRE UNDER THE STARS

STANLEY PARK
MALKIN BOWL
(604) 687-0174

Nightly, between mid-July and mid-August, Stanley Park is transformed into a magical place when the cast of Theatre Under the Stars takes the stage at Malkin Bowl. Usually, the popular troop puts on two different musicals each year accompanied by an amateur (though very capable) orchestra. In the past, audiences young and old have been treated to *West Side Story*, *Hair* and *Oklahoma*. Call ahead to find out what's showing. Don't forget to bring bug repellent and a blanket or two to ward off the nighttime chill.

☞ SEASONS AND TIMES
➤ July 14–Aug 14, Mon–Sat.
Gates open at 7:30 pm. Showtime is 8:30 pm.

☞ COST
➤ Adults $20, youths (12 to 19) $16, children (6 to 12) $10, under 6 free.
Reserved seats $25. Group rates available.

☞ GETTING THERE
➤ By car, take Georgia St. west and follow it to the park. Signs to Malkin Bowl are posted at the park entrance. Pay parking on site. About ten minutes from the Hotel Vancouver.
➤ By public transit, walk north one block to West Pender St. and turn west to take city bus 135 on West Pender and Thurlow (Monday to Saturday, daytime). Take buses 23 or 35 (Sundays, evenings and holidays).
➤ By bicycle, use the car directions.

More Theatre for Kids

There is a slew of theatres and theatrical companies in Vancouver that offer entertainment for families at reasonable prices. For information about upcoming productions, call:

ARTS CLUB THEATRE
1585 JOHNSTON ST.
GRANVILLE ISLAND
(604) 687-1644

AXIS THEATRE COMPANY
1398 CARTWRIGHT ST.
VANCOUVER
(604) 669-0631

Axis, which specializes in performing at schools, features mimes, clowns, puppetry and acrobatics in their shows.

MASSEY THEATRE & PLASKETTE GALLERY
735 - 8TH AVE.
NEW WESTMINSTER
(604) 517-5900

MICHAEL J. FOX THEATRE
7373 MACPHERSON AVE.
BURNABY
(604) 664-8560

QUEEN ELIZABETH THEATRE
649 CAMBIE ST.
VANCOUVER
(604) 665-3050

RICHMOND GATEWAY THEATRE
6500 GILBERT RD.
RICHMOND
(604) 270-1812

SHADBOLT CENTRE FOR THE ARTS
6450 DEER LAKE AVE.
BURNABY
(604) 291-6864

THEATRIX YOUTHEATRE SOCIETY
936 LILLIAN ST.
COQUITLAM
(604) 939-6992

Community Centres

Families with an interest in the arts should check out their local community centre. Many Vancouver-area centres stage monthly performances by children's entertainers that are suitable for youngsters two and up. Better still the shows cost very little to attend. Most centres publish schedules of their upcoming shows and events, or look for one at your library, in the local paper or in the calendar of events distributed by most municipalities to their residents each spring and fall.

Listen to the Music
VANCOUVER SYMPHONY KIDS KONCERTS

ORPHEUM THEATRE
601 SMITHE ST.
VANCOUVER
(604) 684-9100

Don't put off taking your children to the Vancouver Symphony Kid's Koncerts. The popular performances are a great way to introduce them to the joys of classical music and feature excerpts from much-beloved classics such as *Swan Lake, the Nutcracker, William Tell Overture* and *Peter and the Wolf.* The shows, about 45 minutes long, often feature mimes, puppeteers, children's entertainers, ballet dancers and storytellers who interpret the music for audiences. There is no intermission.

☞ **SEASONS AND TIMES**
➙ Oct—Apr, Sun, 2 pm—3 pm.

☞ **COST**
➙ Adults $23.75, youth and students (including university students) $21.50, children (6 months to 12 years) $17.25.
Kids Koncerts package (five shows): Adults $93, children $56.

☞ **GETTING THERE**
➙ By car, take Georgia St. east to Howe St., turn south to Smithe St. and go west. The Orpheum parking lot is at the corner of Seymour and Smithe. Other parking also available close by. About five minutes from the Hotel Vancouver.
➙ On foot, use the car directions.

Seeing the Big Picture
IMAX™ AND
OMNIMAX™ FILMS

Y ou haven't fully enjoyed a big-screen experience until you have watched a film on a towering IMAX™ or OMNIMAX™ screen. For an unforgettable adventure, visit CN IMAX™ Theatre and watch a documentary on the Amazon rainforest or a feature film on kayaking. No matter what show you choose, as soon as the movie starts you will be glued to your seats.

The OMNIMAX™ Theatre at Science World offers science and nature movies on one of the largest dome screens in the world. In this theatre that's equipped with surround sound, everyone will get caught up in the action unfolding on the screen. Be sure to call ahead for ticket prices (they vary depending on the presentation) and scheduling. New and popular shows sell out quickly so be sure to arrive early. Group rates available. Advanced bookings are recommended. Both theatres are wheelchair accessible.

CN IMAX™ THEATRE
201 - 999 CANADA PLACE
VANCOUVER
(604) 682-IMAX (4629) OR 1-800-582-4629

OMNIMAX™ THEATRE
1455 QUEBEC ST.
VANCOUVER
(604) 443-7443

In the Spotlight
KITSILANO SHOWBOAT

2300 CORNWALL AVE. (ADJACENT TO THE KITSILANO POOL)
VANCOUVER
(604) 734-7332

To see Vancouver's up-and-coming performing stars, head to the Kitsilano Showboat, where music, song and dance are staged outdoors on summer evenings. This beachside venue has been a popular destination for families for more than 30 years, and children as young as five have taken to its stage and stolen the show. Show up early if you want a spot on the benches.

☞ **SEASONS AND TIMES**
➤ Late June—late Aug, Mon, Wed, Fri. Shows start at 7:30 pm.

☞ **COST**
➤ Free. Donations accepted.

☞ **GETTING THERE**
➤ By car take Burrard St. south across the Burrard St. Bridge to Cornwall Ave. and go west to Kitsilano Beach Park. Pay parking on site. About 25 minutes from the Hotel Vancouver.
➤ By public transit, take city bus 2 or 22.
➤ By bicycle or on foot, use the Seaside Bicycle Route.

Sensational Sundays
QUEENS PARK BANDSHELL

**BETWEEN 1ST ST. AND 3RD AVE.
NEW WESTMINSTER
(604) 525-0485**

Spend a summer Sunday afternoon having a picnic lunch and enjoying free quality family entertainment at the Queen's Park Bandshell. Music groups, dance troupes, clowns and dancers perform one-hour shows that delight youngsters. Sometimes, kids are invited to participate in the shows.

☞ **SEASONS AND TIMES**
➤ Mid-June—Labour Day Weekend, Sun, 2 pm (cancelled if raining).
☞ **COST**
➤ Free.

☞ **GETTING THERE**

➤ By car, take Seymour St. north to Cordova St. and go east (it merges into Dundas) to Nanaimo St. and turn north to McGill St. Follow McGill east to Hwy.1 and go south. Take the Kensington exit to Canada Way (it becomes 8th Ave.) and head south. Turn east on 3rd Ave. and enter the park. Free parking on site, but come early. About 1 hour from Vancouver.

➤ By public transit, take the SkyTrain from Burrard Station to 22nd St. in New Westminster. Transfer to city bus 155 (towards Coquitlam Recreation Centre) and ask the bus driver to let you off at Queens Park.

Tricks of the Trade
INSTRUCTION IN THE PERFORMING ARTS

A re your children eager to express themselves creatively? You will find all sorts of fun and educational classes geared for kids at the schools listed below.

VANCOUVER ACADEMY OF MUSIC
1270 CHESTNUT ST.
VANCOUVER
(604) 734-2301

T hink your child has what it takes to be the next Mozart? The Vancouver Academy of Music offers a wide variety of classes suitable for kids of all ages and talents. From piano to cello, flute to guitar, the Academy offers lessons for just about any instrument. Register your children for group or private lessons and choose from a range of instructional methods.

The Academy also runs a classical ballet school for children ages 5 to 18. Auditions are required. Classes at the Academy fill quickly. Call for information and reservations. If you would rather watch, there are musical performances throughout the year and a ballet recital once a year. Call the Academy for more information.

VANCOUVER YOUTH THEATRE
200 - 275 E. 8TH AVE.
VANCOUVER
(604) 877-0678

Vancouver Youth Theatre offers courses in drama for individuals ages 6 to 20 taught by professional directors. The company also puts on performances for schools, conferences and the general public. With subjects geared towards children and teens, the youth theatre educates both kids and adults on issues facing young people today. There are summer programs for kids who have been bitten by the acting bug. Call for more information.

EVERGREEN CULTURAL CENTRE
1205 PINETREE WAY
COQUITLAM
(604) 927-6550

Evergreen Cultural Centre offers a wide spectrum of visual and performing arts classes for the whole family. The kids' programs are educational, and geared towards classroom learning. Schools are encouraged to book programs in painting, drawing, sculpture, and drama.

Come join in the fun on the last Sunday of every month when Evergreen offers Family Sundays. Your kids can participate in free workshops on kite making, painting or drawing, and parents are welcome too. There's an arts camp during Spring Break for children 7 to 12. In the fall, Evergreen runs Family Series concerts with quality children's entertainment, such as puppeteers and musicians.

☞ Family Sundays: Last Sunday of every month, 1 pm—4 pm.
Family Series: Varies. Call for schedule.

☞ Family Sundays: Free.
Family Series: Adults $10, children $8.
For ticket information call the box office at 927-6555.

☞ Take Seymour St. north to Cordova St. and go east (it merges with Dundas) to Nanaimo St. Take Nanaimo north to McGill St. and go east to Hwy. 1. and follow it east until the last exit for Port Coquitlam. Take Hwy. 7 (Lougheed Hwy.) north. It becomes Pinetree Way. Pay parking on site. About 60 minutes from the Hotel Vancouver.
Walk north to Hastings St. and take city bus 160 to Pinetree Way and Gilford St.

ARTS UMBRELLA
1286 CARTWRIGHT ST.
VANCOUVER
(604) 681-5268

This school offers 154 classes each week in the performing and visual arts. Children 2 to 18 can take courses in acting, drama, art, photography and sculpture. Children can also participate in the Arts Umbrella's Youth Dance Company or Theatre Company. Call for information on prices and schedules.

CIRKIDS, SCHOOL OF CIRCUS ARTS
5995 PRINCE ALBERT ST.
VANCOUVER
(604) 737-7408

Professional circus performers lead workshops on riding a unicycle, juggling, walking a tightrope and many other neat tricks. For kids ages 6 to 16. Call for information on schedules and prices.

CAROUSEL THEATRE SCHOOL
1411 CARTWRIGHT ST.
GRANVILLE ISLAND
VANCOUVER
(602) 685-6217 (BOX OFFICE) 669-3410 (ADMINISTRATION)

Carousel Theatre School, located at The Waterfront Theatre, offers classes led by professional actors and directors in acting, directing, script writing, designing sets, costume and scenery props for children seven and older. Kids can also take courses to learn about performing monologues, play building, theatre improvisation and theatre games.

The group puts on shows at schools as well as performances for families throughout the year. For more information, call the numbers above.

CEPERLEY PARK PLAYGROUND
SECOND BEACH
STANLEY PARK
(604) 241-9724

On weekday summer evenings, Ceperley Park Playground becomes the place to jive. Dance the night away with free lessons in traditional Scottish dancing, international, ballroom or West African.

☞ Mon: Scottish · (604) 241-9724 or (604) 270-4241
   Tue: International · (604) 736-7873
   Wed: Ballroom · (604) 876-3778
   Thu: West African · (604) 584-5330

LIVING IN CINÉ

I f you don't care much for movies coming out of Hollywood these days, alternate options are increasingly available. Check out a children's film festival or a repertory house near you for entertainment that is affordable and suitable for the whole family.

The National Film Board of Canada

A lthough you can no longer borrow films at the NFB, you can still purchase videos there. Animated shorts, Canadian classics and other interesting and education films are waiting to become part of your movie collection. If you would rather borrow the videos, visit the main branch of the Vancouver Public Library. They have a good selection of NFB titles to choose from.

NATIONAL FILM BOARD OF CANADA
200 - 1385 W. 8TH AVE.
VANCOUVER
(604) 666-3838

VANCOUVER PUBLIC LIBRARY (MAIN BRANCH)
350 W. GEORGIA ST.
VANCOUVER
(604) 331-3600

Repertory Houses

W atching movies on the big screen doesn't have to put a dent in your wallet. Repertory Cinemas may not show the big-name films as soon as first-run the-atres do, but you can't argue with their prices, which are even lower when you purchase a membership.

One- or two-month schedules are available, so you can plan ahead for your night, or nights, out at the movies.

HOLLYWOOD THEATRE
3123 W. BROADWAY, VANCOUVER (604) 738-3211
FEATURES SECOND-RUN MOVIES AT INEXPENSIVE PRICES.

☞ (All prices include two shows.) Tue—Sun: Adults $4.50, seniors and children $3. Mondays, $3.

VARSITY THEATRE
4375 W. 10TH AVE., VANCOUVER (604) 222-2235

☞ Adults $9, students $7.50, children $5. Tuesdays, $5.

DUNBAR THEATRE
4555 DUNBAR ST., VANCOUVER (604) 222-2991

☞ Adults $9, students $7.50 , children $5. Tuesdays, $5.

RIDGE THEATRE
3131 ARBUTUS ST., VANCOUVER (604) 738-6311

☞ First-run movies: Adults $7, children $4.
Double Feature: Adults $5, children $3.
Tuesdays: Adults $5, children $3.

Film Festivals

Reel to Real, a relatively new film festival for youths eight and up, features more than 40 films from 13 countries, including documentaries, animated films and shorts. The festival begins on the first Wednesday in March and runs for four days at the

Norman Rothstein Theatre (950 W. 41st Ave., Vancouver) and the Roundhouse Community Centre (181 Roundhouse Mews, Vancouver). Tickets are priced at $5 per person. For more information, call (604) 224-6162.

Other Places

Café Champlain

CHAMPLAIN HEIGHTS COMMUNITY SCHOOL
6955 FRONTENAC ST.
VANCOUVER
(604) 257-8315

On the last Friday of every month Café Champlain offers patrons an open stage and a featured performer. This kid-friendly venue is perfect for families whatever the children's ages. While you and your older ones sit and listen to music in a cozy atmosphere, the youngsters will be watching videos, playing basketball and making arts and crafts across the hall in the gym that's well-supervised.

☞ Year-round: Last Friday of every month, 7:30 pm—10 pm.

☞ Adults $5, children (2 to 16) $2 (includes access to the gym).

☞ Take Georgia St. east, cross the Georgia Viaduct and exit at Main St. Turn south on Main, continue until 49th St. and turn east to Frontenac St. and drive about two kilometres to Champlain Heights Elementary. Free on site parking. About 50 minutes from the Hotel Vancouver.
Take city bus 8 on Granville St. to 49th St. and Granville, then transfer to the 49 bus (east) and ride it until Frontenac.

Rogue Folk Club

THE WISE HALL
1882 ADANAC ST.
VANCOUVER
(604) 736-3022
WWW.ROGUEFOLK.BC.CA

The Rogue Folk Club features folk performances from around the world. Although much of the content is geared toward adults, this unique club welcomes children too. If a foot-stomping band is playing, everyone can get up and dance. Visit their Web site or check your local newspaper for the dates of performances that the whole family can enjoy together.

☞ By car, take W. Georgia St. east (its name changes to E. Georgia) and drive over the E. Georgia Viaduct. Its name changes to first Prior St. and then Venables St., but continue going east until Victoria Dr. and turn south for one block. Parking on nearby streets. About 30 minutes from the Hotel Vancouver.

By public transit, take city bus 20 from Granville St. Get off at Commercial Dr. and Adanac St.

CHAPTER 7

Animals,
Farms
& Zoos

Introduction

There are many farms around Vancouver, which is great news for folks who enjoy get-aways to the country. Whether your family decides to pick berries by the bushel or hike through a bird sanctuary, there is no shortage of fun things to do in the region surrounding Vancouver. This chapter tells you where you can feed cuddly animals at Maplewood Farm or watch whales splash around at the Vancouver Aquarium. Learn how to ride at Adventures on Horseback or stop in at the Rainforest Reptile Refuge Society to visit with exotic animals. There are also outings to the police stables and seasonal trips to see bald eagles. Other destinations in this chapter include visits to Orphaned Wildlife and Maplewood Conservation area. So pick a spot and head out for a day of family fun.

NOTE

You'll also find animals at the Greater Vancouver Zoological Centre (Chapter 12, page 235).

Pawing around at the SPCA ANNUAL JUNIOR PET SHOW

**KERRISDALE ARENA
5670 EAST BLVD.
VANCOUVER
(604) 599-PAWS (7297)**

I s your pooch a shoo-in to win the cutest puppy contest? Enter your family pet into the annual show put on by PAWS, a volunteer animal shelter, and it might win a prize for the best wagging tail or loudest bark. Cats, rabbits, hamsters and mice are some of the many contestants at this kid-friendly event. But you don't have to own a pet to participate. Watch dogs perform agility or flyball demos, check out the displays or you can attend a workshop on how to care for animals. Kids love eating not-dogs while roaming around making new furry friends. If your children show a keen interest in animals, sign them up for the SPCA youth (8 to 15) club or summer camp that focuses on humane education and animal safety. PAWS also offers year-round programs for schools and there are workshops and animal-friendly preschool programs. Call for more information.

☞ **SEASONS AND TIMES**
➤ Second week in May. (Call for exact times or look in a newspaper.)

☞ **COST**
➤ Free. (Donations accepted.)

☞ **GETTING THERE**
➤ By car, take Burrard St. south across the Burrard St. Bridge to 16th Ave. and turn west. Turn west again at the next set of lights onto Arbutus St. Continue until 37th Ave., turn east for one block and then south onto East Blvd. Free parking on site. About 20 minutes from the Hotel Vancouver.
➤ By public transit, take city bus 16 (Arbutus) south from the corner of Georgia St. and Granville St.

Fishing for Facts at the VANCOUVER AQUARIUM

STANLEY PARK
VANCOUVER
(604) 685-3364
WWW.VANAQUA.ORG.

R ain or shine, the Vancouver Aquarium in Stanley Park is always a great destination for a family outing. Boasting five aquatic habitats including Arctic Canada, the Pacific Northwest, Amazon Rainforest, Tropical Pacific and the Pacific Canadian Pavilion, there are plenty of animals to capture the interest of youngsters.

Explore the waters of Queen Charlotte Sound in a submarine or stop in at the West Coast touch pool to find out what sea urchins feel like. Kids love watching the performing sea otters and dolphins and they can learn about fish through the aquarium's interactive displays. If your children are fascinated with aquatic life, sign them up for the Encounters program that offers them an opportunity to interact with fish and animals. Kids can feed the sharks, participate in the training of killer whales or meet an octopus.

The Aquarium also offers other educational programs for children and adults as well as sleepovers

☞ **SEASONS AND TIMES**

➥ Summer: Late June–early Sept, daily, 9:30 am–7 pm.
Winter: Early Sept–late June, daily, 10 am–5:30 pm.
Christmas and New Year's, noon–5pm.

☞ **COST**

➥ Adults $12.95, youths (13 to 18) $10.95, children (4 to 12) $8.55, under 3 free, families (two adults, three children) $42.95.
Encounters program extra. Memberships available. Group booking and rates available. All major credit cards accepted.

and birthday parties. Call the aquarium or visit its
Web site for details.

☞ **GETTING THERE**

➤ By car, take Georgia St. west and follow it to the park. Signs are posted at
the park entrance. Pay parking on site. About 10 minutes from the Hotel
Vancouver.

By public transit, walk north one block to W. Pender St. and turn west to
catch the city bus 135 at W. Pender and Thurlow (Monday to Saturday, daytime). Take city bus 23 or 35 on Sundays, evenings and holidays.

By bicycle, use the car directions.

☞ **NEARBY**

➤ Stanley Park Zoo and Miniature Railway. Lions Gate Bridge.

☞ **COMMENT**

➤ Plan a 2-hour visit

E-I-E-I-O
CHILDREN'S FARMYARD

STANLEY PARK
(604) 257-8530

For a taste of the country in down-town Vancouver, stop in to see the creatures at Stanley Park's petting zoo. Besides the regular farm animals, you can meet a sheep with four horns and a beard, a don-key, a llama and Shetland ponies. The reptile house is filled with creepy, crawly

☞ **SEASONS AND TIMES**

➤ Summer: June—Sept, daily, 10 am—
5 pm.
Other times: Varies, call for schedule.

☞ **COST**

➤ Farmyard or the Miniature
Railway: Adults $2.50, children
(2 to 12) $1.25, youths (12 to 17)
$1.75, families $5 (two adults and
two children).
Farmyard and Train: Families $8.50.
Group rates available.

snakes and spiders. Don't forget to take a ride on their miniature train. Contact the zoo for details on their special events such as reptile day, a chat with the bee man and Easter Sunday sheep shearing.

 **GETTING THERE**

→ By car, take Georgia St. west and follow it to the park. Signs are posted at the park entrance. Pay parking on site. About 10 minutes from the Hotel Vancouver.

→ By public transit, walk north one block to W. Pender St. and turn west to catch city bus 135 on W. Pender and Thurlow. (Monday to Saturday, daytime). Take city bus 23 or 35 on Sundays, evenings and holidays.

→ By bicycle, use the car directions.

☞ **COMMENT**

→ Plan a 1-hour visit.

Horsing Around at the
VANCOUVER POLICE MOUNTED GUARDS STABLES

601 PIPELINE RD.
STANLEY PARK
(604) 717-2775

☞ **SEASONS AND TIMES**

→ Year-round: Daily, dawn to dusk. Call for a schedule of when the horses will be at the stables.

☞ **COST**

→ Free.

D id you know your family could visit the stables of the Vancouver Mounted Police and learn how rider and horse work together to fight crime? Drop by to meet Pico, Cambie, Buddy, Jedi, Sabre and Justice and their owners, of course. Hear the fascinating history of the mounted police and discover how much time and energy goes in to caring for each horse. Guided tours are offered to groups of five or more.

☞ **GETTING THERE**

➤ By car, take Georgia St. west and follow it to the park. Signs are posted at the park entrance. Pay parking on site. About 10 minutes from the Hotel Vancouver.

➤ By public transit, walk north one block to W. Pender St. and turn west to catch city bus 135 on W. Pender and Thurlow (Monday to Saturday, daytime). Take city bus 23 or 35 on Sundays, evenings and holidays.

➤ By bicycle, use the car directions.

☞ **NEARBY**

➤ Stanley Park farmyard and miniature train, Vancouver Aquarium, Lions Gate Bridge.

☞ **COMMENT**

➤ Plan a 1-hour visit.

❥❥❥

Visiting Feathered Friends at
OWL SANCTUARY

ORPHANED WILDLIFE
3800 72ND ST.
DELTA
(604) 946-3171
WWW.REALM.CA/OWL

Introduce your children to the wonders of wildlife by visiting the Orphaned Wildlife centre (OWL). Created as a rehabilitation and care facility for orphaned and injured birds, OWL has recently opened its doors to the public. With 21 permanent residents and many patients on the mend, the OWL interpretation

☞ **SEASONS AND TIMES**
→ Year-round: Sat—Sun, 10 am—3 pm.

☞ **COST**
→ By donation.

☞ **GETTING THERE**
→ By car, take Granville St. south across the Granville St. Bridge to 16th Ave. and turn east to Oak St. Take Oak south across the Oak St. Bridge to Hwy. 99. and continue south until the Twawwasen/Victoria Exit (second exit after the Deas Tunnel). At the second set of lights, turn east onto Ladner Trunk Rd. (it becomes Hwy. 10). Turn south at 72nd St. Free parking on site. About 1 hour from the Hotel Vancouver.
→ By public transit, walk east on W. Georgia St. to Howe St. and take city bus 601 (South Delta) to the Ladner Exchange. Transfer to bus 318 (Scottsdale) and get off at 72nd St.

☞ **NEARBY**
→ Boundary Bay.

☞ **COMMENT**
→ Plan a 1-hour visit.

centre is a great place to learn about birds of prey and their habitats.

When you arrive at the centre, you will meet Oddey, a friendly barn owl who helps with the educational programs. You can then take a one-hour guided tour of the facility and meet several other owls, hawks, osprey and falcons, see a video and learn about the centre's work. Educational programs are available both on and off-site for schools and communities. Adopt a bird ($20 for one or $30 for a pair in the same cage) and your kids can go home with a photo of the bird they adopted and a letter detailing the bird's background at the centre. Birthday parties can be arranged (and the presents can go towards adopting or sponsoring a bird).

A Taste of the Exotic at the RAINFOREST REPTILE REFUGE SOCIETY

1395 - 176TH ST.
SURREY
(604) 538-1711
WWW.RAINFORESTSCARCH/COM/RRRS

Kids love creepy crawly creatures and that is just what you will find at the Rainforest Reptile Refuge. Filled to the brim with exotic animals, this centre is dedicated to the care, rehabilitation and conservation of unwanted pet shop novelty animals.

Take a tour of the shelter and catch sight of turtles, crocodiles, snakes, lizards and tarantulas. They also have parrots, cockatiels and hedgehogs. Learn about the various habitats these creatures call home and what roles they play within their respective ecosystems. Educational visits for school and community groups are available.

If your kids decide they want their own

☞ **SEASONS AND TIMES**
➙ Summer: Tue—Sun, 10:30 am—4:30 pm (subject to change).
Winter: Fri, Sat, Sun, 10:30 am—4:30 pm.
Weekdays and evenings reserved for pre-booked groups only.

☞ **COST**
➙ Adults $4.50, children (3 to 12) $2.95, under 3 free. Family discounts available.

☞ **GETTING THERE**
➙ By car, take Granville St. south across the Granville St. Bridge to 16th Ave. and turn east to Oak St. Take Oak south across the Oak St. Bridge continuing south Hwy. 99 through the Deas Tunnel (Rte. 99) to Exit 2 (Truck crossing exit). Turn east at the first set of lights, onto 176th St. Then turn north. The shelter is about one kilometre down the road on the left. Free parking on site. About one hour from the Hotel Vancouver.

☞ **COMMENT**
➙Group tours need to pre-book. Plan a 1-hour visit

lizard or spider, why not adopt an animal from the shelter? However, you will not have the responsibility of caring for the pet, since it stays at the centre. Any money you donate is used to provide food and shelter. Your kids will even get a certificate with a photo of their animal to take home and a plaque (bearing the person's name) will be mounted on the animal's enclosure.

Making Tracks to the SERPENTINE FEN NATURE WALK

King George Hwy. and 44th Ave.
Surrey
(604) 582-5222 or 1-800-665-7027

G et out your bird book and binoculars, round up the troops and head out for an amateur bird watching and tracking adventure at Serpentine Fen Naturel Walk. This 80-hectare salt marsh attracts a range of different waterfowl, songbirds and a variety of raptors, such as owls. Follow the well-marked trail to three viewing towers and read the interpretive signs along the way. Other animals live here too, including rabbits, harbour seals and frogs. Pack bug repellent, plenty of water and boots so little feet won't get wet. You can even bring your bikes and cycle along the river dyke.

☞ **SEASONS AND TIMES**
→ Year-round: Daily, dawn to dusk.

☞ **COST**
→ Free.

☞ **GETTING THERE**

➤ By car, take Granville St. south across the Granville St. Bridge to 16th Ave and turn east to Oak St. Take Oak south across the Oak St. Bridge to Hwy. 99 and continue south until the north exit to the King George Hwy. (Hwy 99A). From King George Hwy., turn west onto 44th Ave. and continue to the parking area on the left (closed in the evening). About 50 minutes from the Hotel Vancouver.

➤ By public transit, take the Skytrain from Burrard St. to Surrey Central Station, then transfer to city bus 321 and ride it to 44th Ave.

☞ **COMMENT**

➤ Strollers are only suitable to take on the dykes if the weather is dry.

☞ **SIMILAR ATTRACTION**

➤**Maplewood Conservation Area.** This 5,600-hectare open watershed that's operated by Wild Bird Trust of British Columbia is home to many reptile and mammal species as well as 16 types of dragonflies. Wild Bird Trust offers programs such as Bird Survey and Nature Walk. Call for further information. 2645 Dollarton Hwy., North Vancouver (604) 924-2581.

Riding Tall in the Saddle at
ADVENTURES ON HORSEBACK

9230 LADNER TRUNK RD.
DELTA
(604) 940-8140

Take your little cowpokes out for a day on the trail at this adventure ranch. Ride off into the sunset on an exciting overnight camping trip or canter through the waves at Boundary Bay. Guided trail rides for children 10 and up are available, while littler folk will enjoy supervised riding around the corral. Riding lessons are available.

Helmets are provided, but be sure to wear long pants and running shoes or boots.

☞ **SEASONS AND TIMES**
➤ Year-round: Daily. Call to reserve.

☞ **COST**
➤ Prices start at $50.

☞ **GETTING THERE**
➤ By car, take Granville St. south across the Granville St. Bridge to 16th Ave., turn east and drive to Oak St. Take Oak south across the Oak St. Bridge to Hwy. 99. and continue south until the Twawwasen/Victoria Exit (second exit after the Deas Tunnel). At the second set of lights, turn east onto Ladner Trunk Rd. (it becomes Hwy. 10). Free parking on site. About 50 minutes from the Hotel Vancouver.

➤ By public transit, walk east on W. Georgia St. to Howe St. and take city bus 601 (South Delta) to the Ladner Exchange. Transfer to bus 318 (Scottsdale) and get off at 72nd St.

☞ **NEARBY**
➤Boundary Bay, Delta Museum & Archives, Splashdown Park.

☞ **SIMILAR ATTRACTIONS**
➤ **Riverside Equestrian Centre,** 13751 Garden City, Richmond (604) 271-4186.
➤ **Maynard's Southlands,** 3249 W. 51st Ave., Vancouver (604) 266-6398.
➤ **Shannon Riding School,** 3320 W. 55th Ave., Vancouver (604) 263-8201.

Creatures Great and Small
MAPLEWOOD FARM

405 SEYMOUR RIVER PL.
NORTH VANCOUVER
(604) 929-5610
WWW.MAPLEWOODFARM.BC.CA

Animals and more animals, that's what you will find at this farm. See pigs, horses, rabbits, chickens, turkeys, donkeys and more. Climb up Goat Hill to laze around with some very friendly sheep and goats. Be sure to head to the barn at 1:15 pm for daily milking demonstrations. Maplewood Farm frequently has activities such as sheep shearing and pony rides. Also, there are seasonal events including a fair in September, a pumpkin contest at Halloween and a Christmas carol sing-a-long with the barnyard animals in December. Be sure to call ahead for a schedule of events and times. Birthday parties can be arranged.

☞ **SEASONS AND TIMES**
→ Year-round: Tue—Sun, 10 am—4 pm. Open holiday Mondays only.

☞ **COST**
→ Adults $2.14, children (1 to 16) $1.61, families (up to four members) $6.96.

☞ **GETTING THERE**
→ By car, take Burrard St. north to W. Hastings and turn east. Continue east on W. Hastings (which will become E. Hastings) to Nanaimo St. and then turn north. Follow Nanaimo St. around the bend and turn east onto McGill St. Then follow it to the Second Narrows Bridge. Take the first exit off the bridge onto the Dollarton Hwy. and continue east for about one kilometre. Turn north at Seymour River Place. Free parking on site. About 35 minutes from the Hotel Vancouver.
→ By public transit, take city bus 210 (Upper Lynn Valley) from Burrard St. Skytrain Station to the Phibbs Exchange (bus stop 6) in North Vancouver then transfer to bus 212 (Deep Cove). Get off on the Dollarton Highway by Seymour River Place.

☞ **NEARBY**
➤ Park & Tilford Gardens, Cates Park, Maplewood Conservation Reserve.

☞ **COMMENT**
➤ Plan a 2-hour visit.

☞ **SIMILAR ATTRACTION**
➤ **Bluebell Farm.** Farm tours for the public and school groups in the spring to see baby animals. In the fall you can pick pumpkins. The farm also has ostriches and ostrich eggs. 16913 - 66th Ave., Surrey (604) 574-5345.

Bountiful Harvests
FEASTING ON FARM PRODUCE

Nothing tastes better than produce you pick straight from the plant. Luckily for Vancouver residents, there is an abundance of farms nearby where cityfolk can pick strawberries, blueberries, corn, pumpkins and even choose your own Christmas tree. Some places supply the picking containers, but we recommend you bring your own just in case. Be sure to pack hats, sunscreen and water to keep little helpers hydrated. Call ahead to find out what fruits and veggies are in season and what facilities are available at each farm listed below.

ALDOR ACRES/ANDERSON FARMS
24990 84TH AVE., LANGLEY • (604) 888-0788 OR (604) 530-0704

Easter weekend see baby farm animals. Hayrides in the last week of September to the pumpkin patch. Hayrides to the tree farm in December.

BAKEYS FARM MARKET
5954 RIVER RD., LADNER • (604) 940-2358

A selection of beets, carrots, dill cukes and garlic. Bring your own baskets.

BISSETT FARMS LTD.
2170 WESTHAM ISLAND RD., DELTA • (604) 946-7139

A selection of strawberries, raspberries, blueberries and potatoes.

DRIEDIGER FARMS
23823 - 72ND AVE., LANGLEY • (604) 888-1665

Berries, currants, gooseberries. Closed Sundays.

JOE'S BERRY FARM
10531 GRANVILLE RD., RICHMOND • (604) 278-6308

Blueberries.

KRAUSE BROTHERS FARMS
6179 - 248TH ST., ALDERGROVE • (604) 856-5757

Blueberries, strawberries, blackberries, corn, cucumbers.
Drinks and snacks sold.

WESTHAM ISLAND HERB FARM,
4690 KIRKLAND RD., DELTA • (604) 946-4393

Visit in mid-October and see over 250 carved pumpkins that are lit up each night.

Other Places to Visit

Brackendale Eagle Reserve Society

P.O. BOX 100
BRACKENDALE
(604) 898-9885

For a real thrill, plan a day trip to Brackendale, home of the bald eagles. Between early November and late February you can watch hundreds of bald eagles feasting on salmon in the neighbouring rivers. The weather can be quite wet in these months, so bring waterproof clothing and warm sweaters along with your binoculars.

☞ Take Georgia St. west over the Lions Gate Bridge and take the turn off for West Vancouver. Follow Marine Dr. west to Taylor Way and go north to Hwy. 1 (Upper Levels Highway), go west to Hwy. 99 and follow it north to Brackendale. About one hour from Vancouver.

Call Greyhound Canada for bus directions, (604) 482-8747.

☞ SIMILAR ATTRACTION

➤ **Reifel Bird Sanctuary.** Over 240 bird species have been spotted in this marshland sanctuary. Museum exhibits allow an up-close look at some birds. For best viewing, visit during the spring (March and April) and fall (October to November) migration. See fledglings in spring and snow geese in fall. Westham Island, 5191 Robertson Rd., Delta (604) 946-6980.

CHAPTER 8

green
spaces

Introduction

Parks are natural destinations for families who love the outdoors. Fortunately, green space abounds in and around Vancouver where you and your kids can throw a Frisbee™ or kick a soccer ball around, have a picnic and enjoy the scenery. Some parks provide opportunities of a more exciting variety. At Capilano Regional Park you can walk across a suspension bridge that's 70 metres above ground. Kids won't want to miss Rainbow Playland in Queens Park or rock climbing in the Youth Park at Bear Creek. Visit an authentic Chinese Garden or learn all about plants at Vancouver's Botanical Gardens. Many of the parks listed here also offer swimming, hiking, cycling, horseback riding, and canoeing. Parks allow you to create your own fun, and at the end of the day, that's what family outings are all about.

NOTE

The Greater Vancouver Regional District operates 22 green spaces in the Lower Mainland. For more information, including maps and brochures or to register for an educational program, please contact Greater Vancouver Regional District Parks at 4330 Kingsway, Burnaby (604) 432-6350 or 432-6359.

The following green spaces, which are covered elsewhere in this guide, are also perfect for families:

A Piece of Solitude
IONA BEACH
REGIONAL PARK

GREATER VANCOUVER REGIONAL DISTRICT, PARKS DEPT.
(604) 432-6350 OR (604) 224-5739
WWW.GVRD.BC.CA/PARKS/BRO/PKION.HTML

To leave it all behind, plan to spend a day at Iona Beach Regional Park. Just 40 minutes from downtown, this tranquil spot offers families opportunities for hiking, cycling, in-line skating and sunbathing. Take the kids for a walk out to the jetty and see if you can spot a whale or seals that are rumoured to swim just off its tip. Or, visit the marsh and lake, where over 137 species of birds have been sighted, including herons, owls, ducks and shorebirds. There are interpretive displays about park's ecology and its wildlife on the grounds. Bring your binoculars and bird guides.

A short stroll northwest of the parking lot is the Fraser River, where you can watch barges and tugboats hard at work moving logs to sawmills up the river. There is a sandy beach where kids can build sandcastles and

☞ **SEASONS AND TIMES**
➤ Year-round: Daily, 8 am—dusk.
(Open until 10 pm in summer.)

☞ **COST**
➤ Free.

☞ **GETTING THERE**
➤ By car, take Granville St. south across the Granville St. Bridge and continue until you cross the Arthur Laing Bridge to the airport. Take the Richmond Exit. Turn east at the first set of lights. Then turn north almost immediately for Iona Island and follow the road along the edge of the airport. Free parking on site. About 30 minutes from the Hotel Vancouver.

☞ **NEARBY**
➤ Vancouver International Airport.

you can go swimming between the north and south
arm jetties, although it is unsupervised. Park inter-
preters give tours and there are discovery-oriented
programs for families (call 432-6359).

Cap off your visit by stopping near the
Vancouver airport on your way home. From Grauer
Road, your kids can ogle the airliners flying low
overhead. Don't forget to pack snacks, sunscreen,
hats and liquids when you visit.

A Gem in the City
QUEEN ELIZABETH PARK

33RD AVE. AND CAMBIE ST.
VANCOUVER
(604) 257-8584

☞ **SEASONS AND TIMES**
➤ Park: year-round, daily, dawn—
dusk.
Conservatory: Summer (Apr 1—Oct 1),
Mon—Fri, 9 am—8 pm; weekends,
10 am—9 pm. Winter, daily, 10 am—
5:30 pm.
Pitch and Putt: Call 874-8336.

☞ **COST**
➤ Park access: Free.
Bloedel Conservatory: Adults $3.30,
children (6 to 18) $1.65, under 5 free.
Pitch and Putt: Adults $7.50, youths
(12 and over) $4.30.

An outing to Queen
Elizabeth Park is
one the whole
family will enjoy. Open
year-round, this pretty
park, which is built on an
old rock quarry, features
several attractions including a golf course, tennis
courts and a pitch-and-
putt for children 12 and
over.

In spring, you can
stroll through the park's

spectacular rose gardens, or watch geese swim around the park's ponds. If it is grey or rainy, stop in at the Bloedel Floral Conservatory, a triodetic dome full of lush greenery, fish ponds and over 100 tropical birds. Come winter, bring your toboggans. The park is renowned for its great sledding hills as much as it is for its beauti-

☞ **GETTING THERE**
➤ By car, take Georgia St. east to Cambie St., turn north and cross the Cambie St. Bridge. Stay on Cambie until 29th Ave. and turn east. The park will be on your right. Pay parking on site. About 25 minutes from the Hotel Vancouver.
➤ By public transit, take city bus 15 on Burrard St.

☞ **NEARBY**
➤ Nat Bailey Stadium.

ful vistas of the city, ocean and mountains.

There is a cafeteria on site and plenty of choice spots where you can have a picnic. Bring water, sunscreen and hats for everyone in summer, and bundle up in winter.

Wide Open Spaces
JERICHO PARK AND BEACH

3941 POINT GREY RD.
VANCOUVER
(604) 257-8400 (VANCOUVER PARKS)

Feeding the ducks in Jericho Park is a popular pastime for many Vancouver families. If you visit during spring, be sure to keep an eye out for ducklings and goslings that live in the park's pond. The trails that lead away from the pond will bring you into marshes where other wildlife such as rabbits, birds, and occasionally eagles, reside.

Animals aren't the only creatures to enjoy this park. Little tikes love riding their bikes on the path that borders the ocean. The Jericho Yacht Club, along the way, is a great spot to sit and watch wind-surfers, kayakers and sailors on the water. If fishing is more your style, bring your rods and head out onto the pier. Children love spinning the ship's wheel found there. Kayaks and canoes can be rented at the Yacht Club in summer.

Bring a kite when you come. The winds off the ocean make this park perfect for flying kites. Towels and bathing suits in the summer are a must. The beach is clean and lifeguards are on duty. You'll also find volleyball courts and barbecues close by. Be sure to bring sunscreen, water, hats for everyone and a blanket to sit on. A concession stand serves drinks and snacks. Or, pack a picnic. There are tables where you can eat and take in the view. The park is the site for the family-friendly Vancouver Folk Music Festival (page 220) in mid-July.

☞ **SEASONS AND TIMES**
➤ Year-round: Daily, dawn—dusk.

☞ **COST**
➤ Free.

☞ **GETTING THERE**
➤ By car, take Burrard St. south across the Burrard St. Bridge. to Cornwall Ave. and head west. Continue along Cornwall (its name changes to Point Grey Ave.). The road makes a sharp turn south to Alma St., but stay west until the very end of Point Grey Rd. Pay parking on site. About 20 minutes from the Hotel Vancouver.
➤ By public transit, take city bus 4 from Granville St. Disembark at 4th Ave. and Alma walk north three blocks to Point Grey Rd., then west to the park.
➤ By bicycle, use the Seaside Bicycle Route.

On the Path to
PACIFIC SPIRIT
REGIONAL PARK

4915 WEST 16TH AVE.
VANCOUVER
(604) 224-5739

Vancouverites love exploring Pacific Spirit Park, whether on foot, by bike or on horseback. Extending over 706 hectares of forested land, this park has 40 kilometres of trails leading to ravines, marshes, bogs and rocky beaches. You'll find maps at the Interpretive Centre on 16th Avenue showing you the routes to follow. If you book in advance, a park interpreter will lead your crew on a hands-on nature trip describing plant and animal life along the way (224-5739). Once you have a destination, spray on some bug repellent and head outdoors. Everyone should keep their eyes peeled for mice, racoons and chipmunks. You might even spot an eagle or two if you're lucky.

Don't miss out on visiting Camosun Bog. One of the oldest bogs in

☞ **SEASONS AND TIMES**
➝ Year-round: Daily. The park opens at 8 am though closing times vary monthly, so call ahead.

☞ **COST**
➝ Free.

☞ **GETTING THERE**
➝ By car take Granville St. south across the Granville St. Bridge and exit on Fir St. Go south on Fir to 16th Ave. and turn west. Continue along 16th until the entrance to the park at Camosun St. Park on nearby streets, or at the parking lot (free) at the information centre. About 30 minutes from the Hotel Vancouver.
➝ By public transit, take city bus 8 at Granville Mall. Disembark at King Edward Ave. and Granville and transfer to bus 25, which will drop you at 16th Ave. and Camosun.

☞ **NEARBY**
➝ University of British Columbia.

the Lower Mainland, this soggy sphagnum bog is one of 132 ecological reserves in British Columbia and preserves 89 hectares of second growth forest.

If you plan to swim at one of the beaches, please note they are unsupervised and an adult must accompany children. The park has nature programs and special events for all ages. Call 432-6359 for a schedule.

Finery and Flowers
VANDUSEN BOTANICAL GARDENS

5251 Oak St.
Vancouver
(604) 878-9274
www.vandusengarden.org

K ids can develop their green thumbs at VanDusen Botanical Gardens, which has over 7,500 different plants from six continents. With waterfalls and man-made ponds, floating bridges and landscaped rocks, the gardens offer visitors a tropical getaway when the weather is cool and grey.

☞ **Seasons and Times**
→ Year-round: Opens at 10 am. Call for closing hours, as they vary monthly.

☞ **Cost**
→ Summer: Adults $5.50, youths (6 to 18) $2.75, families $11. Winter: Adults $2.75, youths (6 to 18) $1.50, families $5.50. Memberships available.

Interactive displays help guide you through the gardens, where you can stroll through a 20-minute overview of what VanDusen has to offer, or spend a few hours examining the greenery in depth. While older kids will enjoy following the self-guided tour for children, their younger siblings will love visiting the pond where they can spot resident frogs, turtles, waterspiders and fish.

Be sure your visit includes the Elizabethan maze and the Children's Garden, a delight for kids of all ages. Budding botanists will find many books at the library to pore through. Guided tours are offered daily between April and October (year-round on Sundays at 2 pm). For group reservations or to book a cart tour for those with limited mobility, call 257-

> ☞ **GETTING THERE**
> ➤ By car take Granville St. south across the Granville St. Bridge and continue south until 37th Ave. then turn east to VanDusen. Free parking on site. About 15 minutes from the Hotel Vancouver.
> ➤ By public transit, walk west on Georgia St. to Burrard St and take city bus 17 at Burrard and Pender St.

8666. VanDusen has seasonal educational programs for schools and summer children's nature programs for community centres and youth groups. See the Web site for details. There are also family adventure programs ongoing throughout the year. Call 878-5860 for information and to make reservations.

Feeding Time at
DR. SUN YAT-SEN
CLASSICAL CHINESE
GARDENS

578 CARRALL ST.
VANCOUVER
(604) 662-3207

Tucked away behind a courtyard amidst the hustle and bustle of Chinatown, the beautifully landscaped gardens of Dr. Sun Yat-Sen are the only full-sized classical gardens of their kind outside of China. The plants found here among the jade-green pools and sculpted rocks were selected for their ancient symbolic meanings and include banana trees and bamboo groves. The best time for kids' visits is when it's lunchtime for the carp, koi and goldfish that live in the garden's pond. After the gong is rung, the hungry fish swim to the surface waiting to be fed. The staff will be happy to give you a tour and explain the various Chinese customs associated with designing and

☞ **SEASONS AND TIMES**
➤ Spring (May 1—June 14): Daily, 10 am—6 pm.
Summer (June 15—Sept 30): Daily, 9:30 am—7 pm.
Winter (Oct 1—Apr 30): Daily, 10 am—4:30 pm.

☞ **COST**
➤ Adults $6.50, children (5 to 17) $4, families $15.

☞ **GETTING THERE**
➤ By car, take Burrard St. north to W. Pender St. and head east until Carrall St. Pay parking across the street. About ten minutes from the Hotel Vancouver.
➤ By public transit, walk north on Burrard St. to Pender St. and take city bus 19 or 22.

☞ **NEARBY**
➤ Chinese Cultural Centre, Chinatown.

maintaining the gardens. A complementary tea is served to visitors. Guided tours run once an hour during July and August. For tours during the rest of the year, call for a schedule and times. Groups of ten or more should book ahead.

Delightfully Inviting
QUEENS PARK

CORNER OF 1ST ST. AND 3RD AVE.
NEW WESTMINSTER
(604) 524-9796

L ooking for a place to let your kids run rampant? Give Queens Park a try. This popular family destination has plenty of grassy areas that are good for hitting a ball or playing a game of tag.

Rainbow Playland is the park's big attraction for kids who like sliding, jumping, swinging and climbing. If it's a warm day, pack towels and bathing suits for the spray pool. Animal lovers will want to visit the children's petting farm (525-0485) and see all their favourite farm friends such as rabbits, goats, sheep, calves and chickens. Depending on the season, you can take in a hockey game at Queens Park Arena or stop by the large gymnasium to register your kids for volleyball, soccer, gymnastics or tumbling pro-

☞ **SEASONS AND TIMES**
→ Park: Year-round, daily, dawn—dusk.
Children's farm: Victoria Day—Labour Day, daily, 10 am—5:30 pm.
Spray Park: Early May—Late Sept, daily, 10 am—5:30 pm, depending on the weather.

☞ **COST**
→ Free.

grams. If you like music, plan on visiting the park for its Sensational Sunday concerts, a series of free shows offered on Sundays at 2 pm (June to August). There are also tennis courts and an art gallery in the park.

☞ **GETTING THERE**

➤ By car, take Seymour St. north to Cordova St. (it eventually merges into Dundas) and go east to Nanaimo. Take Nanaimo north to McGill St., turn east and access Hwy. 1 (Trans-Canada Hwy.) eastbound. Take the Kensington South Exit (Canada Way) and follow it east to New Westminster and then turn north on 3rd Ave. to the park. Free parking on site. About 50 minutes from the Hotel Vancouver.

➤ By public transit, take the Skytrain from Burrard Station and get off at 22nd St. in New Westminster. Transfer to city bus 155 (towards Coquitlam Recreation Centre). Ask the bus driver to let you off at the park.

A Family Outing to
DEER LAKE PARK

6450 DEER LAKE AVE.
BURNABY
(604) 294-7450
WWW.BURNABYPARKSREC.ORG/DEER/DEER.HTML

An oasis of greenery amidst downtown Burnaby, Deer Lake Park is a fun place to take little urban explorers. With a lake for boating and canoeing, a playground, a vintage carousel, meadows, marshland and hiking trails, this park is well equipped for families who like being outdoors. Bring binoculars for

---

☞ **SEASONS AND TIMES**

➤ Year-round: Daily, dawn—dusk.

☞ **COST**

➤ Free.

birdwatching and keep an eye out for beavers and frogs. But there's more, including art exhibits at Ceperley House, flower festivals at Century Gardens and art activities at the Shadbolt Centre, which also sells snacks and drinks. The park is also the site of several annual events, including outdoor concerts put on by the Vancouver Symphony Orchestra.

It can get muddy during the rainy season, so be sure to dress appropriately.

☞ **GETTING THERE**

➤ By car, take Seymour St. north to Cordova St. and go east (it merges into Dundas) to Nanaimo St. Take Nanaimo north to McGill St., turn east and access Hwy. 1 (Trans-Canada Hwy.). Take the Kensington South Exit (Canada Way) and follow the signs to Deer Lake Park. Free parking on site. About 35 minutes from Hotel Vancouver.

➤ By public transit, walk north for three blocks to Hastings St., then take city bus 123 or the Skytrain to Metrotown, and transfer to bus 144.

☞ **NEARBY**

➤ Burnaby Village Heritage Museum, Shadbolt Centre, Burnaby Lake Regional Park and Nature House.

Weathering Heights
CAPILANO REGIONAL PARK

3735 CAPILANO RD.
NORTH VANCOUVER
(604) 985-7474
WWW.CAPBRIDGE.COM

Hovering 70 metres above the Capilano River, the Capilano Suspension Bridge is one of Vancouver's oldest and most popular attractions. Originally built in 1889 out of hemp rope and cedar planks, the present version is much, much stronger. If you are brave enough to cross the bridge (hold onto your child's hand when you do), you'll find hours of fun activities awaiting on the other side. Pick up special passports at the park entrance that kids can have stamped at every attraction they visit.

At the Story Centre, guides dressed in 19th century clothing tell you all about Capilano's fascinating history. You can examine hands-on historical artifacts or listen to an audio show. The Big House has displays on how totem poles are carved and at Totem Park there's a collection of over 25 totems dating from the 1930s. Before you set off to explore the trails that loop through the old growth forests, be sure to stop at the Living Forest, where interactive photo displays, models of bugs and fun facts will teach kids and adults about forest ecology. There are free park tours offered daily between May and October. Or, wander on the trails yourself and see a waterfall, a miner's cabin, flora and trout ponds.

☞ SEASONS AND TIMES
→Summer: Daily, 8 am—dusk.
Winter: Daily, 9 am—5 pm.

☞ COST
→ Adults $9.95, children (6 to 12) $3.15, under 6 free.
All major credit cards and traveller's cheques accepted.

☞ GETTING THERE
→ By car, take Georgia St. west through Stanley Park and cross the Lions Gate Bridge. Take the North Vancouver Exit and at the first set of traffic lights turn north onto Capilano Rd. Pay parking on site. About 15 minutes from the Hotel Vancouver.
→ By public transit, take city bus 246 heading west on Georgia St. Disembark at Ridgewood Dr. and Capilano Rd. and walk north one block on Capilano Rd.

☞ NEARBY
→ Capilano Salmon Hatchery, Cleveland Dam, Capilano River Regional Park, Grouse Mountain.

☞ COMMENT
→ The park is wheelchair and stroller accessible, however strollers are not allowed on the bridge. Staff will store them for you.

There's daily entertainment in the summer in front of the Big House, featuring the North Wind Dancers who perform native songs and dances at 11:30 am, 2:30 pm and 6:30 pm. Three on-site restaurants serve meals to hungry visitors.

Migrating to
BEAR CREEK PARK

CORNER OF KING GEORGE HWY. AND 88TH AVE.
SURREY
(604) 501-5050
WWW.CITY.SURREY.BC.CA

T here's something fun for every member of your family here, whether it's hiking, biking, picnicking or exploring the park's many other attractions. Younger children will love playing at the adventure playground while older kids will want to hang out at Youth Park, which has a climbing wall, a skateboard park, roller hockey and a basketball court. There are also sports fields for soccer, football or a game of tag. The outdoor pool and spray park offer a refreshing break from the summer heat.

If it's nature you're after, head to Bear Creek, where interpretive signs provide information about coho salmon, which navigate these waters during their migration. Save time for the spectacular flower gardens and for the kids to have a ride on the miniature train (call 501-1232).

☞ **SEASONS AND TIMES**
↝Year-round: Daily, dawn—dusk.
☞ **COST**
↝ Park: Free. Miniature Train: Adults $2, children $1.50.

☞ **GETTING THERE**

➤ By car, take Granville St. south across the Granville St. Bridge to 16th
Ave. and turn east to Oak St. Follow Oak south across the Oak St. Bridge
and continue on until you see a sign for Hwy 91. and North Delta. Take this
exit and follow the road to the Alex Fraser Bridge. Take the Nordel Way
Exit east (it becomes 88th Ave. in Delta) and follow it east to 120th St. Free
parking on site. About one hour from the Hotel Vancouver.

➤ By public transit, take the Burrard St. Skytrain to Surrey Central and
transfer to bus 321 (White Rock).

☞ **NEARBY**

➤ Surrey Arts Centre and Gallery.

Fun and Games
RICHMOND NATURE PARK

11851 WESTMINSTER HWY.
RICHMOND
(604) 273-7015

Begin your visit to Richmond Nature Park at
The Nature House, where hands-on games
and activities will teach kids about their natural surroundings. Exhibits about tree frogs, bee-
hives, snakes, stick insects and deer mice round out
the fun things to explore. That done, head outside
and hit the trails. Be sure to pick up a nature trail
guide before you go so kids can refer to it along the
way (the booklet has historical and factual information about the park's forest and bogs).

Make your second stop at the wildlife garden. Kids
will love the brightly coloured flowers and other

exhibits found here. Then head to the bogs, where there are several easy trails for kids to navigate. There is a boardwalk around a small duck pond that makes it easy for pushing strollers.

The park runs several nature programs during the year offering kids the chance to learn about birding, insects and bogs. They'll even get to build their own birdhouses (registration is required). Richmond Nature Park has guided nature walks every Sunday at 2 pm. Don't miss the Cranberry Harvest Festival in October or June's Slugfest. Call for a schedule and times.

☞ **SEASONS AND TIMES**
→ Park: Year-round, dawn—dusk. Nature House: Mon—Thu, 8:30 am— 5 pm.

☞ **COST**
→ Free.

☞ **GETTING THERE**
→ Take Granville St. south across the Granville St. Bridge to 41st Ave. Turn east on 41st to Oak St. then go south across the Oak St. Bridge to Hwy. 99 S. Take the Westminster Hwy. Exit and then go east to the park. Free parking on site. About 50 minutes from the Hotel Vancouver.
→ By public transit, walk east to Howe St. and take any Richmond bus 400 series to the Richmond Exchange at Richmond Centre. Transfer to bus 405. Get off at Westminster Hwy. and No. 5 Rd.

☞ **SIMILAR ATTRACTION**
→ **Burnaby Nature House,** 9146 Avalon Ave., Burnaby (604) 520-6442.

Other Green Spaces

Lighthouse Park

BEACON LANE
WEST VANCOUVER
(604) 925-7200

H ave you ever wanted to see the inside of a lighthouse? Then take a trip to Lighthouse Park
where Point Atkinson lighthouse, built in 1912, sits
atop rocky bluffs overlooking the Pacific Ocean.

The park features 76 hectares of green space,
with many trails that boast some of Canada's largest
trees, such as Douglas fir, hemlock and western red
cedar. The main trail that leads to the water is best
suited for walking with young children. Bring a picnic and eat it beneath the lighthouse.

West Vancouver Parks and Recreation offers
educational nature programs at Lighthouse Park
year-round. In the summer, kids can participate in
hands-on nature programs at the Phyll Mundy
Nature House every Sunday between 2 and 4 pm.

☞   Year-round: Daily, dawn—dusk.

☞   Free.

☞   Take W. Georgia St. west, cross the Lions Gate Bridge and
take the West Vancouver Exit. Drive west along Marine Dr. past
Ambleside and then the Dundarave shopping centres. Free parking. About 45 minutes from the Hotel Vancouver.

Cates Park

**OFF THE 200 BLOCK DOLLARTON HWY.
NORTH VANCOUVER
(604) 990-3800
WWW.DISTRICT.NORTH-VAN.BC**

I n a quiet corner of Burrard Inlet, this pretty seaside park is the perfect place to get away for quiet picnics, swimming and other fun outdoors.

Boasting sandy beaches (supervised July 1 to Labour Day weekend), Cates Park also has tennis courts, two playgrounds and hiking trails through the forest. A display of First Nations' totem poles and a 15-metre-long canoe depict the rich history of British Columbia's native peoples.

During the summer on Saturday evenings between 5:30 pm and 8:30 pm, there are free musical concerts. A concession stand serves snacks and drinks for hungry tummies.

☞ Year-round: Daily, dawn—dusk.

☞ Free.

☞ Take Burrard St. north to W. Hastings and go east to Nanaimo St. Turn north to McGill St. Go east and cross the Second Narrows Bridge. Take the first exit and continue east on Dollarton Hwy. to the park. Free parking on site. About 50 minutes from the Hotel Vancouver.

By public transit, take city bus 210 (Upper Lynn Valley), from Burrard St. Skytrain Station to the Phibbs Exchange (bus stop 6) in North Vancouver. Transfer to bus 212 (Deep Cove) and ride it to Cates Park.

CHAPTER 9

HISTORICAL
SITES

Introduction

Vancouver has evolved from a wild-west town in the late 1800s to a bustling metropolis. For kids, there is no better way to learn about Vancouver's rich history than to experience it at the heritage and historical sites in this chapter. At the Gulf of Georgia Cannery, you can learn about the history of the salmon canning industry first-hand. B.C. residents made significant sacrifices during the First and Second World Wars, and they are chronicled at the Museum of The Royal Westminster Regiment. At Burnaby Village Museum and Fort Langley National Historic Site, visitors can step back in time and experience life in the 1800s. And there's more. London Heritage Farm, Christ Church Cathedral, Britannia Heritage Shipyard, B.C Museum of Mining, Old Hastings Mill Store and Gastown have their own stories to tell that will not only engage your children, but will keep them asking for more.

Fortified History at FORT LANGLEY NATIONAL HISTORIC SITE

23433 MAVIS ST.
FORT LANGLEY
(604) 513-4777
WWW.HARBOUR.COM/PARKSCAN/FL/

There's plenty of hands-on fun at Fort Langley, which is the site where British Columbia was proclaimed a colony in the late 1850s. Kids can participate in activities such as baking bannock, panning for gold and blacksmithing. Staff in period costume will tell you about the fort, which became a Hudson's Bay Company Trading Post and was also a major stop for prospectors on their way to the Fraser and Cariboo Rivers during the gold rush.

Visitors can tour historic buildings, including an original storehouse from the 1840s. Stop in at the theatre building and watch a video about Fort Langley's history. You can bring a picnic and lunch on

☞ **SEASONS AND TIMES**
➛ Mar 1—Oct 31: Daily, 10 am—5 pm.

☞ **COST**
➛ Adults $4, seniors (over 64) $3, children (6 to 16) $2, under 6 free, families $10.
Group rates available. Reservations required for groups of ten or more.

☞ **GETTING THERE**
➛ By car, take Seymour St. north to Cordova St. and go east to Nanaimo St. (Cordova merges into Dundas). Turn north to McGill St. and drive east to access Hwy 1. E (Trans-Canada Hwy.) Take the 232nd St. N. Exit and continue to Glover Rd. and turn north. Follow the signs to Fort Langley and then turn east onto Mavis St. to the fort. Free parking on site. About one hour from the Hotel Vancouver.

NEARBY
→ Langley Centennial Museum,
Farm Machinery and Agricultural
Museum, Canadian Museum of
Flight, Derby Reach Regional Park,
Village of Fort Langley.

☞ **COMMENT**
→ Plan a 2-hour visit.

the grounds, or dine at one of the charming restaurants in the rural village of Fort Langley nearby, with its artists' studios and curio shops.

Fort Langley offers special events throughout the year, such as Brigade Days in August and a Cranberry Festival at Thanksgiving. It also has educational programs for schools about the gold rush, the First Nations and other subjects. Call for details and prices.

Digging for Facts at the B.C. MUSEUM OF MINING

OFF HWY. 99
BRITANNIA BEACH
(604) 688-8735 (TOLL FREE)
WWW.MOUNTAIN-INTER.NET/BCMM

P ick a clear day to drive to this museum and you'll be treated to some of British Columbia's most spectacular coastal scenery along the Sea to Sky Highway. The museum, located at an abandoned copper mine, is a B.C. Historic Landmark.

Interpretive staff dressed as miners will lead you on a two-hour journey of the site, beginning with a video presentation about Britannia's history as a copper-mining town. Afterward, you'll be given a hard hat to wear for your tour around the Industrial Yard. The Mining House has three levels of displays to see, including documents, old photographs, exhibits about rocks and minerals, and there's an overview of B.C. mining history.

The highlight of the visit will be boarding the miniature train to explore a mine that's almost 400 metres underground. If you have younger children, tell them what to expect beforehand, so they won't be frightened in the mine. The tour also includes visiting three early diamond drills and Mill No. 3, built to refine Britannia's ore. Later, kids can try panning for gold at the mine's gold recovery area.

☞ SEASONS AND TIMES
→ Spring (early May—late June) and Fall (early Sept—early Oct): Wed—Sun, 10 am—4:30 pm.
Summer (early July—Labour Day): Daily, 10 am—4:30 pm.
Winter: School tours only, reservations required. Call for a schedule of opening hours during spring break.

☞ COST
→ Adults $9.50, youths and students $7.50, under 5 free, families $34.
Gold panning: $3.50.
Group (20 or more) rates available. Call (604) 688-8735 ext. 222 for reservations.

☞ GETTING THERE
→ By car, take Georgia St. west across the Lions Gate Bridge and take the turnoff for West Vancouver. Follow Marine Dr. west to Taylor Way and turn north to Hwy. 1 (Upper Levels Hwy.). Drive west along Hwy. 1, which becomes 99 N. (Sea to Sky), and continue on to Britannia Beach. Look for the huge dump truck that's parked outside the mine. Free parking on site. About one hour from the Hotel Vancouver.

☞ COMMENT
→ A park and a picnic area are adjacent to the museum. Bring a sweater for the underground segment. Plan a 3-hour visit.

A Walk through Time
BURNABY VILLAGE MUSEUM

6501 DEER LAKE AVE.
BURNABY
(604) 293-6500 (RECORDED INFORMATION) OR (604) 293-6501
WWW.BURNABY.PARKSREC.ORG

I nstead of just hearing about the good old days, children can actually live them at the Burnaby Village Museum, a five-hectare open-air site offering visitors the chance to experience life in the Lower Mainland during the early 1900s. The village has many turn-of-the-century buildings, such as a one-roomed schoolhouse, a bank, a gas station, a barber-shop and several homes. You can talk to the costumed staff who are hard at work in the bakery and the black-smith's shop, or visit the popular printing de-monstration in the Burnaby Post Print Shop.

Next, head to the Don Wrigley Pavilion for a ride on the antique carousel. Bring a lunch and have a picnic on the grass, or eat it at one of the many tables located on the grounds. Plan your visit during Christmas or Easter and your kids can enjoy story-telling, a magic show and other special activities. On Canada Day there's free admission, a parade, a cake and games for families. In September, there's the Fall Fair with tasty wares and a petting zoo. Birthday party packages are available.

☞ **SEASONS AND TIMES**
➤ Late Apr—mid-Sept and late Nov—early Jan: Daily, 11 am—4:30 pm (call to confirm).
Closed Christmas Eve and Christmas Day.

☞ **COST**
➤ Adults $6.45, youths (13 to 18) $4.45, children (6 to 12) $3.85, families (up to five members) $3.85 per person. Carousel: $1.

☞ **GETTING THERE**

→ By car, take Seymour St. north to Cordova St (it will become Dundas) and turn east to Nanaimo St. Go north to McGill St. then head east and access Hwy. 1 (Trans-Canada Hwy.). Take Hwy. 1 east to Kensington S. Exit 33 (Canada Way) and turn west onto Canada Way and follow the signs. Free parking on site. About 30 minutes from the Hotel Vancouver.

→ By public transit, take the Skytrain to Metrotown Centre, transfer to the SFU bus 144 and ride it to the Burnaby Village stop.

☞ **NEARBY**

→ Shadbolt Centre of the Arts, Ceperley House, Deer Lake Park.

☞ **COMMENT**

→ Plan a 3-hour visit.

On Cannery Row
GULF OF GEORGIA
CANNERY

12138 - 4TH AVE.
RICHMOND
(604) 664-9009
WWW.HARBOUR.COM/PARKSCAN/GGC/

At the beginning of the 20th century, Steveston was the busiest fishing port in the world and its cannery, which packed more than 195,000 cases a year, the leading producer of canned salmon in B.C. Today, the cannery is a dynamic fishing museum with hands-on displays and interactive exhibits that are devoted

☞ **SEASONS AND TIMES**

→Spring (early Apr—late May) and Fall (early Sept—late Oct): Thu—Mon, 10 am—5 pm.
Summer (early June—early Sept): Daily, 10 am—5 pm.

☞ **COST**

→ Adults $5, youths (6 to 16) $2.50, families $12.50.

☞ **GETTING THERE**

→ By car, take Granville St. south across the Granville St. Bridge continuing on until 16th Ave. Turn east to Oak St. then go south crossing the Oak St. Bridge and access Hwy. 99. Take Hwy. 99 south and get off at the Steveston Hwy. Exit. Go west on Steveston to No. 1 Rd., then south to Chatham St. and turn west to 4th Ave. Free parking on nearby streets. About 40 minutes from the Hotel Vancouver.

→ By public transit, walk east on W. Georgia St. and take city bus 401, 406 or 407 south on Howe St. The bus will drop you at Chatham St. and 2nd Ave. Walk west two blocks.

☞ **NEARBY**

→ Steveston Village, Garry Point Park, Steveston Museum, London Heritage Farm, Fisherman's Wharf, Historic Tram 1220.

☞ **COMMENT**

→ Plan a 2-hour visit.

to educating visitors about the west coast fishing industry.

There is historic machinery, models and over 10,000 artifacts to examine. Kids can pick up rubber fish; weigh themselves on a fish scale; punch a time card; or step inside a cramped wheelhouse and experience life aboard a fishing boat. The small tank inside the cannery allows future anglers to hone their skills (rods and reels supplied), and the Boiler House Theatre has a film about the fishing industry.

The museum has a variety of educational programs for school groups, including a shadow puppet workshop for kindergarten students. Special events are ongoing throughout the year. Check the Web site above or call the museum for schedules and times. The Ice House Discovery room, scheduled to open in Spring 2000, will feature 3-D puzzles, role-playing activities and other fun, interactive games for kids.

Old-time Homestead
LONDON HERITAGE FARM

6511 DYKE RD.
RICHMOND
(604) 271-5220

This heritage farmhouse is fully restored to its condition in the 1880s complete with a horseshoe pitch, a tool museum and farm equipment from the era.

Visitors are invited to go on a tour of the house and examine the period furniture and memorabilia that belonged to the London family. Outside, there are herb and flower gardens to visit and, later, you can inspect a 1901 buggy. Bring a picnic and lunch on the grounds, or order afternoon tea and scones at one of the dining rooms in the house (open in the summer; suggested donation $3).

The farm has several annual events. The most popular one for families is the Family Farm and Craft Fair (mid-August), with its pony rides, miniature train ride and wood carving demonstrations. You'll find

☞ **SEASONS AND TIMES**
➤ Summer: July—Aug, daily, 10 am—4 pm.
Winter: Sept—June, weekends and holidays, noon—4 pm.

☞ **COST**
➤ Free.

☞ **GETTING THERE**
➤ By car, take Granville St. south across the Granville St. Bridge and continue on to 16th Ave. Turn east to Oak St. then go south crossing the Oak St. Bridge and access Hwy. 99 S. Get off at the Steveston Hwy. Exit and continue west along Steveston to No. 2 Rd. and turn south. Continue to its end and then turn east on London Rd. and south on Dyke Rd. Free parking on site. About 40 minutes from the Hotel Vancouver.

activities during Halloween, Mother's Day and Easter teas and a Christmas Craft Fair in November. Group tours are available. For more information, call the number listed above.

☞ **NEARBY**
→ Steveston Historical Village, Gulf of Georgia Cannery, Steveston Museum, Chinese Buddist Temple, West Coast Seeds Demonstration and Research Garden.

☞ **COMMENT**
→ Plan a 2-hour visit.

☞ **SIMILAR ATTRACTIONS**
→ **Historic Stewart Farmhouse**, Elgin Heritage Park, 13723 Crescent Rd., Surrey (604) 502-6456.

→ **Irving House Historic Centre**, 302 Royal Ave., New Westminister (604) 527-4640. www.city.new-westminster.loc.ca/cityhall/museum

Set Sail into History
BRITANNIA HERITAGE SHIPYARD

5180 WESTWATER DR.
RICHMOND
(604) 718-8050
WWW.STEVESTON.BC.CA

To learn how Vancouver-area history is tied to the sea, visit the Britannia Heritage Shipyard. This historic site has displays showing visitors how local fisherman plied their trade and the role residents played in maintaining the Anglo British Columbia's fishing fleet.

You can go on a guided tour or stroll along the boardwalk at your own pace (information packets are available at Murakami's Visitor Centre). Nine of the buildings are restored and open to the public. There's a collection of old boats and dugout canoe skiffs to view and wood carvings. You'll find photographs and other exhibits at the Machinery Room and interactive activities for kids. Workers are often building and repairing boats at the shipyard, and they might ask you to give them a hand. Feel like paddling? You can rent kayaks and canoes, and guided canoe tours (reservations required) are offered.

Special events are going on all the time. B.C. River Day in September features children's activities, ethnic performances

☞ SEASONS AND TIMES

➤ Spring (Early Mar—Early May): Wed—Sat, 10 am—4 pm; Sun, noon—4 pm.
Summer: (Early May—Early Sept): Tue—Sun, 10 am—4 pm.
Winter: (Early Sept—Early Mar): Sat, 10 am—4 pm; Sun, noon—4 pm.
Subject to change. Please call to confirm.

☞ COST

➤ By donation.

☞ GETTING THERE

➤ By car, take Georgia St. east to Howe St. and go south across the Granville St. Bridge. Continue south on Granville to 41st Ave. and then turn east to Oak St. Take Oak south across the Oak St. Bridge to access Hwy. 99 S. Take the Steveston Hwy. Exit and go west on Steveston until Railway Ave. Go south on Railway and follow the signs. Free parking on site. About 40 minutes from the Hotel Vancouver.
➤ By public transit, take city bus 401, 403, 406 or 407 to Richmond Centre. Transfer to bus 402 and ride it to Railway St. and Moncton St. The shipyard is a short walk from there.

☞ COMMENT

➤ Plan a 1-hour visit.

and tasty barbecued fish. Looking for some evening entertainment? There are sea shanty concerts at the shipyard (second Tuesday of every month: 7:30 to 9:30 pm). Creative birthday packages with model ship building are offered (also available for school groups).

Atten-shun
MUSEUM OF THE ROYAL WESTMINSTER REGIMENT

530 QUEENS AVE.
NEW WESTMINSTER
(604) 526-5116

☞ **SEASONS AND TIMES**

→ Year-round: Daily, Tue and Thu, 11 am—3 pm (Thu evening from 7 pm—9 pm.). Closed holidays.

☞ **COST**

→ Free.

☞ **GETTING THERE**

→ By car, take Seymour St. north to Cordova St (it will become Dundas) and turn east to Nanaimo St. Go north to McGill St. then head east and access Hwy. 1 (Trans-Canada Hwy.). Take Hwy. 1 east to the New Westminster Exit and proceed to Columbia St., which is in downtown New Westminster. Turn north on 6th St. and continue a few blocks uphill to Queens Ave., just past City Hall. Free parking on site. About 45 minutes from the Hotel Vancouver.

→ By public transit, walk north on Burrard St. to the Skytrain station and take the Skytrain to New Westminster Station. Transfer to bus 106 and ride it to 6th St. and Queens.

Visitors are invited to delve into military history at the Museum of the Royal Westminster Regiment. Housed in an armory gunroom built in 1895, the museum has displays detailing the sacrifices that Vancouver-area men and women made during the First and Second World Wars. In the viewing collection there are rifles and other artifacts such as grenades, shells, gas masks, telescopes and radios. Kids can examine uniforms and there's a scale model of a motor battalion.

> ☞ **NEARBY**
> →Queens Park, Irving House Historic Centre & New Westminster Museum & Archives, Samson V. Maritime Museum, Fraser River Discovery Centre, Canadian Lacrosse Hall of Fame.
>
> ☞ **COMMENT**
> → Plan a 1-hour visit.
>
> ☞ **SIMILAR ATTRACTION**
> → **Fifteenth Field Artillery Regiment Museum** (page 50). 2025 West 11th Avenue, Vancouver (604) 666-4370.

Other Historical Sites

Christ Church Cathedral

690 BURRARD ST.
VANCOUVER
(604) 682- 3848
WWW.CATHEDRAL.VANCOUVER.BC.CA

Built in 1889, Christ Church Cathedral is Vancouver's oldest stone church. Constructed in the Gothic style, arched windows and flying buttresses adorn its exterior. Step inside, however, and you cannot help but note the clearly Canadian touches, such as the Douglas fir and cedar ceiling beams.

Ask your kids if they can identify the biblical stories depicted in the beautiful stained-glass windows, or spot the organ pipes and the Bishop's chair on the high altar. Carols and Gregorian chants are frequently performed here. Call for information.

☞ Year-round: Mon—Fri, 10 am—4 pm.
Services Sunday morning.

☞ By donation.

☞ The Church is across the road from the Hotel Vancouver on
the northeast side of W. Georgia St.

SIMILAR ATTRACTIONS

St. Andrew Wesley Church, 1012 Nelson St., Vancouver (604) 683-4574.

Holy Rosary Cathedral, 646 Richards St., Vancouver (604) 682-6774.

Gastown

BETWEEN HASTINGS ST., WATER ST., HOMER ST. AND COLUMBIA ST.

G astown is Vancouver's oldest district. Although
parts of the area were destroyed by fire in 1886,
today the restored Victorian buildings lining the
cobblestone streets house boutiques, cafés, restaurants and galleries. Among the highlights for kids
will be seeing the famous Gastown Steam Clock
(corner of Cambie Street and Water Street), which
emits a plume of steam when the clock whistles the
hour. There's a collection of railcars and cabooses
that kids love to inspect behind Water Street.

☞ Year-round: Daily.

☞ Free.

☞ Take W. Georgia St. east to Seymour St. and turn north to
Hastings St. Look for street parking. About ten minutes from the
Hotel Vancouver.
Take city bus 1 northbound on Burrard St. Or, take the Skytrain
to the Waterfront Station.

Old Hastings Mill Store Museum
1575 ALMA RD.
VANCOUVER
(604) 734-1212

A s Vancouver's oldest building, the Old Hastings Mill Store is quite a sight to behold. One of the only buildings to survive Vancouver's great fire in 1886, the museum is filled to the brim with all sorts of artifacts, from furniture to tools to fossils.

Visitors of all ages love poring over items that are heaped in every corner of this museum, including old cameras, clocks, whale vertebrae, antique vacuum cleaners, fish skin boots and snowshoe mats made from porcupine needles. Kids love looking at the collection of antique china dolls and clothing from the early 1900s.

☞   Winter: Sat—Sun, 1 pm—4 pm.
Summer: Tue—Sun, 11 am—4 pm.

☞   By donation.

☞   Take Burrard St. south across the Burrard St. Bridge and exit to Cornwall Ave. Head west until Point Grey Ave. Turn west onto Point Grey and continue until Alma St., then head south until 4th Ave. and turn west. Free parking on nearby streets. About 20 minutes from the Hotel Vancouver.
Take city bus 4 from Granville St. and get off at 4th Ave. and Alma. Walk north three blocks to Point Grey Rd., then walk west.

CHAPTER 10

GETTING THERE IS HALF THE FUN

Introduction

In the case of some family outings, the journey is the destination. In other words, the act of boating, walking, cycling, skating or travelling by train is a large part of what makes the day enjoyable for you and your kids. If you like to cycle, in-line skate or go for long walks, Vancouver's Seaside Bicycle Routes are a network of scenic paths that offer the opportunity to take many interesting side trips along the way. If it's water you love, why not ride a ferry around Vancouver's waterways, or book your passage aboard a cruise boat or an old-fashioned paddlewheeler? Train lovers will enjoy a ride on the West Coast Express commuter train or the Royal Hudson steam engine. This chapter also lists other interesting ways of getting around, including touring by bus and trolley or going on a kayaking expedition. There's also some information about Vancouver's public transportation system. So check your energy levels and then rev up for a day of non-stop fun.

NOTE

You'll find these other fun ways to travel elsewhere in this guide:

Helicopter tours (Chapter 1, page 24.)

Driving a go-cart (Chapter 4, page 106)

Horseback riding (Chapter 7, page 153)

Walking across the Capilano Suspension Bridge (Chapter 8, page 171)

Renting a boat at Britannia Heritage Shipyard (Chapter 9, page 188)

Ahoy Matey!
AQUABUS FERRIES LTD.

1617 FORESHORE WALK
VANCOUVER
(604) 689-5858
WWW.AQUABUS.BC.CA

Aquabus, a small passenger ferry service operating in False Creek, is a fun way for families to take in some of Vancouver's sights. Friendly to cyclists, in-line skaters and even pets, this ferry offers a continuous service with stops at the foot of Hornby Street, Granville Island, Yaletown, the Science Centre and Stamp's Landing. Kids can wave at the sailboats and kayakers, while parents take in views of the cityscape. Keep an eye out for harbour seals splashing about in the water. Aquabus Ferries Ltd. also offers mini-cruises year-round on False Creek that depart daily from the Arts Club Theatre on Granville Island. The tours feature a running commentary on the points of interest and depart every 15 minutes. No reservations are necessary.

☞ **SEASONS AND TIMES**

➤ Year-round: Daily, 7 am–10 pm (until 8 pm in winter).

☞ **COST**

➤ Ferry (one way): Adults $2, seniors and children (4 to 12) $1, under 4 free. Cruises (25 or 40 minutes): Adults $6 or $8, seniors $4 or $6, children (4 to 12) $3 or $5, under 4 free.

☞ **GETTING THERE**

➤ By car, take Burrard St. north to Nelson St., turn east to Granville St. and drive south across the Granville St. Bridge. Turn west on 4th Ave. and follow the posted signs to Granville Island. Free and pay parking on site. On summer weekends, look for street parking and walk to the island. About 20 minutes from the Hotel Vancouver.

➤ By public transit, take city bus 50 south on Granville Mall.

➤ By bicycle, take the Seaside Bicycle Route.

☞ **SIMILAR ATTRACTIONS**

➤ **False Creek Ferries**, 1804 Boatlift Lane, Vancouver
(604) 684-7781.

➤ **B.C. Ferry Corporation.** Offers day trips and longer voyages.
Ride to Vancouver Island or the Gulf Islands. 1-888-223-3779
http://bcferries.bc.ca

➤ **Albion Ferry.** Free passage from Albion to Fort Langley. Dock
of Fort Langley (604) 467-7298.

➤ **Barnston Island Ferry** (604) 681-5199.

Finding Your Sea Legs
HARBOUR CRUISES

1 DENMAN ST.
VANCOUVER
(604) 688-7246 OR 1-800-663-1500
WWW.BOATCRUISES.COM

Ever thought about taking your kids on a cruise? Harbour Cruises has a one-hour tour of Vancouver Harbour that's very popular with families. While your guide tells you about the sights, the boat will bring you to within hailing distance of the Lions Gate Bridge, Gastown, Stanley Park and other local attractions. If you have older children, they might like going on a Sunset Dinner Cruise, which includes a meal and live entertain-

☞ **SEASONS AND TIMES**
➤ Mid-May—mid-Sept: Daily.
Harbour Cruise: Departs at 11:30 am,
1 pm and 2:30 pm.
Sunset Cruise: 7 pm—10 pm.
Reservations are required.

☞ **COST**
➤ Harbour Cruise: Adults $18,
youths (12 to 17) $15, children
(5 to 11) $6, under 5 free.
Sunset Cruise: $59.99 per person,
under 5 free.

ment. Harbour Cruises offers cruises to other destinations as well, including a Boat/Train combination to Howe Sound. For more information and reservations, call the numbers given above.

☞ **GETTING THERE**

→ By car, take Burrard St. north to Georgia St. and go west to Denman St. Harbour Cruises is located next to Stanley Park. Pay parking on site. About five minutes from the Hotel Vancouver.

→ By public transit, take city buses 240, 246, 250 or 251 on W. Georgia St. On foot, use the car directions. It's about a ten-minute walk.

Rolling Down the River
PADDLEWHEELER RIVER ADVENTURES

810 QUAYSIDE DR.
NEW WESTMINSTER
(604) 525-4465 OR **1-877-825-1302**
WWW.VANCOUVERPADDLEWHEELER.COM

These old-fashioned paddlewheelers are great fun for kids. River Adventures offers several cruise packages including the Fort Langley Adventure Cruise, with an hour and a half stopover at Fort Langley. You can also take tours along the Fraser River (bring your binoculars), Douglas Island or the New

---

☞ **SEASONS AND TIMES**

→ Year-round, varies with package. Call for a schedule and reservations.

☞ **COST**

→ Varies depending on package. Fort Langley Tour: (breakfast and lunch included): Adults $89.95, seniors and students (12 and up) $79.95, children (6 to 12) $39.95, under 5 free, families (two adults and two children) $199.95.

Westminster Harbour. The company also runs a Christmas Cruise, a Mother's Day Brunch Cruise, a High Tea Cruise and luncheon cruises with live music. Trips with themes can be arranged.

☞ **GETTING THERE**

→ By car, take Seymour St. north to Cordova (it eventually merges into Dundas) and go east to Nanaimo St. Take Nanaimo north to McGill St. and go east to Hwy. 1 (Trans-Canada Hwy.). Continue going east on Hwy. 1 until the Willingdon Exit. Turn east and continue along Canada Way (it eventually becomes 8th St.) to the New Westminster Quay. Pay parking on site. About one hour from the Hotel Vancouver.

→ By public transit, take the Skytrain from Burrard St. Station to New Westminster Quay.

☞ **SIMILAR ATTRACTION**

→ **Starline Tours.** Offers a variety of tours including a Mystery Cruise, a Harrison Hot Springs Tour, a Fraser River Exploration Cruise and a Sea Lions Tour. 13942 - 96th Ave., Surrey (604) 522-3506 or (604) 272-9187 . www.starlinetours.bc.ca

---

Exploring Vancouver by PUBLIC TRANSIT

COAST MOUNTAIN BUS COMPANY LTD.
VANCOUVER REGIONAL TRANSIT SYSTEM
(604) 521-0400 (CUSTOMER INFORMATION)
WWW.CMBUSLINK.COM

Vancouver's public transportation system makes it easy for tourists and residents alike to get to many of the attractions around the city. Bus, Skytrain and Seabus schedules can be obtained from the company's Web site or you can also call the phone number listed above for detailed directions from your location. Buses require exact change and if you need to transfer to another bus remember to take a transfer ticket. Transfers are also accepted on Seabuses and Skytrains and are valid for 90 minutes.

SEABUS
WATERFRONT AT THE FOOT OF CORDOVA ST. AND GRANVILLE ST.

T his passenger catamaran connects downtown Vancouver with the North Shore, departing every 15 to 30 minutes. The ride across Vancouver Harbour is just over 12 minutes, which is enough to keep the kids' attention without being too long. Bikes are allowed on board. The Seabus connects to a local bus service at the Lonsdale Quay in North Vancouver. To get to the Seabus Terminal in Vancouver by car or on foot, take Burrard St. north to Cordova St. and turn east to Granville St.

☞ Year-round: Mon—Sat, 6 am—1 am; Sundays and holidays, 8 am—11:30 pm. See Web site for departure times.

SKYTRAIN
WATERFRONT STATION

T his computer-operated train is a great way to start an outing. Fast and exciting, riding the Skytrain is a treat for any kid. Trains depart every 2 to 5 minutes and it takes 40 minutes to travel from one end of the line at Waterfront Station to King George Station at the other. The 20 stops along the way will get you to many of the places listed in this guidebook quickly and easily.

☞ Year-round. Departure and arrival times vary for each station. See the Web site for details.

THE BUS

The Coastal Mountain Bus company operates 833 buses and 244 trolleys that travel across 1,800 square kilometres of the Vancouver area. Many routes connect with the Skytrain and Seabus, making the bus a safe and convenient way to get around town.

> ☞ Year-round: Mon—Fri, 4 am—3:30 am; weekends and holidays, 5 am—1 am.
>
> ☞ **COST**
> Bus, Seabus and Skytrain: The fares depend on time of day and distance travelled. Tickets and FareSaver Cards can be purchased at Seven Elevens, Safeways, Scotia Banks, and some Mac's, Moneymarts and London Drugs stores. Fares listed below are for travel through one zone only. See Web site for details about travelling through two or three zones.
> Regular Fare: Adults $1.50, seniors, students (14 to 19) and children (5 to 13) $1.
> Monthly FareCards: Adults $54, seniors, students (14 to 19) and children (5 to 13) $35.
> Daypass Fare: Adults $6, seniors, students (14 to 19) and children (5 to 13) $4.
> FareSaver Tickets (booklets of 10 tickets): Adults $13.75, seniors, students (14 to 19) and children (5 to 13) $10.

Riding in Style
THE VANCOUVER TROLLEY COMPANY

875 TERMINAL AVE.
VANCOUVER
(604) 801-5515 OR 1-888-451-5581
WWW.VANCOUVERTROLLEY.COM

K ids of all ages love riding trolleys, so why not take advantage of the Vancouver Trolley Company's "hop on, hop off" service and set your own pace when taking in Vancouver's sights. There are 16 stops along the route, including Gastown, Canada Place, the Vancouver Aquarium and Granville Island, and you can get on or get off the trolley at any of them. The trolleys are scheduled to go by each stop at about 30-minute intervals, so you can ride the rails all day long and catch some of Vancouver's main attractions, too. Tickets can be purchased when you board and are good for one day. Strollers are allowed on the trolleys. Group charters are available for parties and other special events.

☞ **SEASONS AND TIMES**
Year-round: Daily, 9 am—6 pm.
The last tour leaves Gastown at 4 pm and arrives back at 6 pm.

☞ **COST**
Adults $22, children (4 to 12) $10, under 4 free.

The Wheels on the Bus Go Round and Round
BUS TOURS

Nothing beats a bus tour if you want an overview of Vancouver-area attractions. You'll get an introduction to Stanley Park, Granville Island, Gastown and other points of interest. Landsea Tours has specialty bus tours that run to Victoria and Whistler in addition to its local tours. The Gray Line of Vancouver offers passenger excursions that last from two to eight hours. Popular with families is its "hop on, hop off" tour. Passengers can leave the tour at designated stops and spend time exploring the sights. Tickets, which entitle their bearers to resume the tour on a later bus, can be used over two days.

GRAY LINE OF VANCOUVER
255 EAST 1ST AVE.
VANCOUVER
(604) 879-3363 OR 1-800-667-0882
WWW.GRAYLINE.CA/VANCOUVER

See Vancouver's sights by day or by night. Stay in town, or head out to Whistler, Vancouver Island, Seattle or the Rocky Mountains. Ride the Decker/Trolley Loop service and get on or off at any one of 27 different points of interest around the city. Kids just love riding the double-decker buses, so gear up for an afternoon of fun aboard a bus.

☞ **SEASONS AND TIMES**

→ Some tours operate year-round, others run between Spring and Fall only. Call for a schedule and departure times.

☞ **COST**

→ Prices vary with tour.
Decker/Trolley Loop: Adults $23.36, seniors $22.43, children (5 to 12) $13.08. Tickets are valid for the day of purchase and the following day only.

LANDSEA TOURS
875 TERMINAL AVE.
VANCOUVER
(604) 255-7272 OR 1-887- 669-2277
WWW.VANCOUVERTOURS.COM

L andsea Tours offers five different narrated bus tours. Ride the Vancouver City Highlights (Tour 1) and visit Gastown, Granville Island, Chinatown and Stanley Park, among other attractions. Tour 2 takes visitors to Grouse Mountain and the Capilano Suspension Bridge. For something a little different, sign your family up for Landsea's Native Heritage Cultural Tour, where you will see an authentic long house and totem poles, eat a traditional native meal and even get to try your hand at weaving cedar bark. Landsea Tours also runs trips to Victoria and Whistler Mountain. Complimentary pick-up and return to all downtown hotels.

☞ **SEASONS AND TIMES**

→Year-round: Varies with tour. Tour 1: Early Jan—Late Dec, daily, 9:30 am and 2 pm. Call for details or visit the Web site.

☞ **COST**

→ Varies between $37 to $104 (Adult Fare) depending on the tour. Tour 1: Adults $37, seniors $34, children $22.

☞ **SIMILAR ATTRACTION**

Pacific Coach Lines, 210 - 1150 Station St., Vancouver (604) 662-7575.

Riding the Rails
WEST COAST EXPRESS

WATERFRONT STATION
THE FOOT OF GRANVILLE ST. AND CORDOVA ST.
VANCOUVER
(604) 488-8906
WWW.WESTCOASTEXPRESS.COM

☞ **SEASONS AND TIMES**
➤ Year-round: Mon—Fri, 5:30 am—9 am and 3:50 pm—7:30 pm. Times vary at each station. See Web site for details.

☞ **COST**
➤ Varies according to distance travelled. Tickets for seniors and children are half the price of adult fares. One way fare: Adults $3 to $7. Weekly fare: Adults $27 to $63. 28-day pass: Adults $90 to $210.

☞ **GETTING THERE**
➤ On foot, walk east along Georgia St. to Granville St., turn north and continue on until Cordova St. It's about a ten-minute walk from the Hotel Vancouver.

More than five million people have used the West Coast Express commuter train since it began operating in 1995. Linking outlying communities such as Mission, Maple Ridge, Pitt Meadows, Port Coquitlam and Port Moody to downtown, this train is a great way to take in the scenery surrounding Vancouver. Bicycles are allowed on board and there's a snack bar to satisfy hungry little tummies.

Full Steam Ahead
THE ROYAL HUDSON

B.C. Rail Station
1311 W. 1st St.
North Vancouver
(604) 984-5246 or 1-800-663-8238
www.bcrail.com/bcrpass/bcrhuson.htm

E veryone will have a tough time resisting a ride on this shiny steam train. Hop aboard the Royal Hudson and puff along past the ocean, waterfalls, mountains and the rugged cliffs of Howe Sound. Pack a lunch to eat on board, or visit the old-fashioned Parlour Car for an afternoon snack. Kids love meeting Bunker Bear, the train's mascot, and don't be shy to ask the friendly staff about the points of interest along the way. They are full of interesting tidbits about the area and its history. The two-hour journey ends in Squamish, with a one-hour layover before the train returns to Vancouver. That will leave you with just enough time to visit the West

☞ **Seasons and Times**
➤ Early May—late Sept: Wed—Sun, departs at 10 am.

☞ **Cost**
➤ Round Trip: Adults $48, seniors (over 59) and youths (12 to 18) $41, children (5 to 11) $12.75, under 5 free. Train/Boat: Adults $69.50, seniors (over 59) and youths (12 to 18) $64.15, children (5 to 11) $23, under 5 free.

☞ **Getting There**
➤ By car, take Georgia St. west and cross the Lions Gate Bridge. Take the North Vancouver Exit and head east along Marine Dr. to Pemberton Ave. and turn south. The station is on your left. Pay parking lot and street parking available. About 30 minutes from the Hotel Vancouver.
➤ By public transit, catch the Royal Hudson Bus that leaves from Stadium Station, Wednesday to Friday at 8:50 am and weekends at 8:30 am.

☞ **Comment**
➤ B.C. Rail has trains to other destinations, including Whistler, The Cariboo, Lillooet, The Rockies and Prince George. Call for more information.

Coast Railway Heritage Park, which has over 50 vintage railway cars to investigate. Admission to this museum is included in the price of your train ticket. You can return to Vancouver on a boat with prior arrangement.

Be Your Own Tour Guide
CYCLING IN VANCOUVER

BICYCLE HOTLINE: **(604) 871-6070**
WWW.CITY.VANCOUVER.BC.CA/CYCLING

The Vancouver Bicycling Network provides safe routes for cyclists throughout the city. Currently six routes covering 35 kilometres are available for families who love to pedal their way around town: Adanac Bikeway, Ontario Bikeway, Off-Broadway Bikeway, Cypress Bikeway, Lakewood Bikeway and the Heather Bikeway (for route maps, visit the Web site). If you prefer a scenic ride, try the Seaside Bicycle Route, a 15-kilometre path that runs beside the water from the University of British Columbia to English Bay in the West End. Or, ride along the seawall in Stanley Park, although it gets busy on weekends. The city requires all bicyclists to wear helmets and to have a warning bell on their bike.

If you plan to cycle with young children, you can rent trail-a-bikes and children's bike seats at the locations below. Then strap on your helmets and start pedalling.

BAYSHORE BICYCLE AND ROLLERBLADE RENTALS
745 DENMAN ST.
VANCOUVER
(604) 688-2453
WWW.GLOBALYNX.NET/BAYSHORE

SPOKES BICYCLE RENTAL
1798 W. GEORGIA ST.
VANCOUVER
(604) 688-5141

DENMAN BIKE SHOP
718 DENMAN ST.
VANCOUVER
(604) 685-9755

Pulling Together
CANOEING AND KAYAKING

ECOMARINE OCEAN KAYAK CENTRE
1668 DURANLEAU ST.
GRANVILLE ISLAND
VANCOUVER
(604) 689-7575 (RENTALS), (604) 689-7520 (SCHOOL)
OR 1-888-4-CKAYAK (1-888-425-2925)
WWW.ECOMARINE.COM

For an extra special treat, why not take the family canoeing around False Creek? Ecomarine Ocean Kayak Centre has canoes and kayaks that you can rent by the hour or the day. They also operate a kayaking school where experienced instructors will teach

☞ **SEASONS AND TIMES**
➤ (Granville Island Store)
Winter: Early Jan—late Apr, daily, 10 am—6 pm.
Spring: May, daily, 9 am—6 pm (Thu and Fri until 9 pm).
Summer: Early June—early Sept, daily, 9 am—6 pm (Thu, Fri and Sat until 9 pm).
Fall: Early Sept—early Jan, Tue—Sun, 10 am—6 pm.
Rental hours depend on daylight. Call to confirm.

enthusiasts of every level the finer points of paddling. Beginners are welcome. Ecomarine operates a second kayak rental at Jericho Beach Park (May to September), adjacent to the Jericho Sailing Club. Paddles and lifejackets that are equipped with whistles are included in the rental price.

☞ COST

→ Double Kayaks $34 (two hours), $48 (four hours), $64 per day.
Single Kayaks $24 (two hours), $34 (four hours), $44 per day.
Lessons: $49 (three hours), $149 (full day).
Season's passes are available.

☞ GETTING THERE

→ By car, take Burrard St. north to Nelson St., turn east to Granville St. and drive south across the Granville St. Bridge. Turn west on 4th Ave. and follow the posted signs to Granville Island. Free and pay parking on site. On summer weekends, look for street parking and walk to the island. About 20 minutes from the Hotel Vancouver.
→ By public transit, take city bus 50 south on Granville Mall.
→ By bicycle, take the Seaside Bicycle Route.

☞ SIMILAR ATTRACTION

→ Deep Cove Canoe and Kayak, Beachfront, North Vancouver (604) 929-2268 www.deepcovekayak.com

---

Other Ways of Getting Around Vancouver

River Rafting

White water rafting is an exciting way for families to spend time together. Here is a listing of places around the Lower Mainland offering rafting for families.

CHILLIWACK RIVER RAFTING ADVENTURES
49704 CHILLIWACK LAKE RD.
CHILLIWACK
(604) 874-5542
WWW.DOWCO.COM/CHILLIWACKRAFTING

REO RAFTING ADVENTURE RESORT
845 SPENCE WAY
ANMORE
(604) 461-7238

WHISTLER RIVER ADVENTURES
1-604-932-3532 OR TOLL FREE 1-888-932-3532
WWW.WHISTLER-RIVER-ADV.COM

The Lookout at Harbour Centre

555 WEST HASTINGS ST.
VANCOUVER
(604) 689-0421
WWW.HARBOURCENTRETOWER.COM

Most kids should get a charge riding an elevator that's enclosed in glass. At Harbour Centre they can travel all the way up to the Lookout and have a clear view of the boats in the harbour below. You'll find displays throughout the Lookout featuring lots of interesting trivia about Vancouver.

☞ Summer: Daily, 8:30 am—10:30 pm.
Winter: Daily, 9 am—9 pm.

☞ Adults $8, children $5, families $22.

Plane Spotting

Everyone loves watching planes, so why not take a drive out to the Vancouver airport to catch sight of some of the great silver birds taking off and landing? For the best views, park on Grauer Road, which connects Iona Island to the Vancouver Airport.

☞ Take Granville St. south and cross the Arthur Laing Bridge to the airport. Take the Richmond Exit from the bridge and turn east at the first set of lights, then turn north almost immediately for Iona Island. Follow Grauer Rd. and look for a safe place to park.

Port of Vancouver

VANTERM PUBLIC VIEWING CENTRE
1300 STEWARD ST. (NORTH FOOT OF CLARK DR.)
(604) 665-9179 OR (604) 665-9179
WWW.PORTVANCOUVER.COM

T ake the kids to the Vanterm Public Viewing Centre where they can see a container terminal in operation and get a close-up view of barges, ships and the bustling port activity. Vanterm has interactive video games and puzzles for solving at its observation deck on the fourth floor. Guided educational tours of the port are offered to all school levels (minimum of ten people).

☞ Year-round: Mon—Fri, 9 am—12 pm and 1 pm—4 pm.

☞ Free.

☞ Take Burrard St. north to W. Hastings then go east until Clark Dr. and turn north.

CHAPTER 11

Favourite Festivals

Introduction

Vancouver is famous for its festivals. From Canada Day parties to the Chinese New Year, Vancouverites find a reason to celebrate year-round. This chapter lists the area's most popular festivals, including the Vancouver International Children's Festival and the Alcan Dragon Boat Festival. In summer, pack a picnic supper and head to the beach for Symphony of Fire's pyrotechnics display. If you like midway rides, fireworks and musical performances, check out the Pacific National Exhibition, the Vancouver Folk Festival or the Point Grey Fiesta Days and Parade. In fact, Vancouver has so many parades, fairs and other spectacles we couldn't fit them all into this chapter. So be sure to check out the Directory of Events for more listings. Then pull out your calendars and start planning for the days of fun ahead.

Child's Play
THE VANCOUVER INTERNATIONAL CHILDREN'S FESTIVAL

VANIER PARK
NORTH OF CORNWALL AVE. ON CHESTNUT ST.
VANCOUVER
(604) 708-5655
WWW.YOUNGARTS.CA

This week-long festival held in late spring has been a family favourite since it began in 1978. Little wonder. The event features a solid lineup of popular Canadian and international children's entertainers who perform theatre, puppetry, music and dance for audiences, under a cluster of candy cane striped tents. In the past, headline acts have included Fred Penner, Raffi and the New Shanghai Circus.

Between shows, roving performers, storytellers and face painters will keep the children entertained. There are

☞ **SEASONS AND TIMES**
➜ Starts on the last Monday in May and runs for seven days.

☞ **COST**
➜ Site admission: $5 per person, under 18 months free.
Concert tickets: $7 to $13 (includes site admission), under 18 months free. Tickets for the shows usually go on sale in late March. The demand for them is high, so buy early. Call 280-4444.

☞ **GETTING THERE**
➜ By car, take Burrard St. south across the Burrard St. Bridge to Cornwall Ave. Turn north on Cypress St. (it's the second exit) and continue to the park. Limited free parking on site. About ten minutes from the Hotel Vancouver.
➜ By public transit, take city buses 2 or 22 south on Burrard to Cornwall and Cypress and walk north for a few minutes.
➜ By bike or on foot, take the Seaside Bicycle Route.

also organized games and activities throughout the day, as well as creative and educational workshops offering kids hands-on instruction in drawing, sculpting with clay, dance, music and much, much more. At mealtimes, you'll find food concessions on site and there are picnic tables for those who bring their lunch. Make sure everyone has rubber boots as the grounds can be muddy.

Power and Passion
THE ALCAN DRAGON BOAT FESTIVAL

PLAZA OF NATIONS AND FALSE CREEK
750 PACIFIC BLVD.
VANCOUVER
(604) 688-2382
WWW.CANADADRAGONBOAT.COM

If you've never seen a dragon boat race, you're in for a treat. Watching 22 paddlers pull together as one and ma-neuver their large boat along the race course is exciting to see. Your whole family will want to cheer for the racers. Dragon boat festivals maintain a Chinese tradition that's 3,000 years old, and the one in Vancouver is renowned for its multicultural flavour. Teams come from all over the world to compete against one another at False Creek. However, boat races aren't the only attraction at the festival. It also boasts an international food festival featuring yummy snacks and there are daily cooking demonstrations. You'll also want to check out the performers who roam the Plaza of the Nations putting on shows for the crowds. Kids will find craft making, interactive science displays and other educational activities at Exhibition Hall.

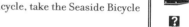 **GETTING THERE**

→ By car, take W. Georgia St. east to Cambie St. Turn south to Pacific Blvd. and drive east to the Plaza of Nations. It's on the right. Pay parking on site. About ten minutes from the Hotel Vancouver.

→ By public transit, take the Skytrain from the Burrard St. Station to the Stadium Station. Walk down the stairs and head south toward GM Place.

→ By bicycle, take the Seaside Bicycle Route.

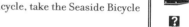 **NEARBY**

→ GM Place, B.C. Place Stadium, B.C. Sports Hall of Fame and Museum, Science World, Score Virtual SportsWorld

 COMMENT

→ You can view the races for free from Science World and other vantage points along False Creek.

In Your Neighbourhood
POINT GREY FIESTA DAYS AND PARADE

W. 10TH AVE. (BETWEEN BLANCA ST. AND DISCOVERY ST.)
VANCOUVER
(604) 257-8140 (WEST POINT GREY COMMUNITY CENTRE)

☞ **SEASONS AND TIMES**
→ The third Saturday in June.
Parade: 10 am.
Trimble Park: 11 am—4 pm.

☞ **COST**
→ Free. There is a charge for rides and games.

☞ **GETTING THERE**
→ By car, take Burrard St. south across the Burrard St. Bridge, bear left at the first set of lights and continue south on Burrard until 12th Ave. Go west on 12th (it eventually becomes 10th Ave.) until Discovery St. and look for street parking. About 25 minutes from the Hotel Vancouver.
→ By public transit, walk east to Granville St. and take city bus 10 (UBC) southbound to 10th Ave. and Discovery.

☞ **NEARBY**
→ University of British Columbia, Pacific Spirit Park, Jericho Beach Park.

☞ **COMMENT**
→ Plan a half-day visit.

Like many neighbourboods in Vancouver, Point Grey has its own summer festival. What sets Fiesta Days apart, however, is a lively, community parade that kicks off the celebrations. Leading the procession on their motorcycles are members of the Vancouver Police Team. Their well-honed riding drills are spectacular, captivating even the youngest members in the audience. Next, you'll see an array of colourful floats and marching bands and even a cavalcade of antique cars. For the best view of the parade arrive early and stake out a spot curbside. It starts at 10 am on Blanca Street and moves east on 10th Avenue to Discovery Street.

When the parade ends, head to Trimble Park for an afternoon of fun that includes live performances, pony rides, carnival games, lucky dips and more. There are concession stands serving munchies at mealtime. You'll also find a playground, a wading pool and spots for sitting out of the direct sun. Pack liquids to keep everyone hydrated, and bring a blanket to spread on the grass.

All the World's a Stage
BARD ON THE BEACH

VANIER PARK
NORTH OF CORNWALL AVE. ON CHESTNUT ST.
VANCOUVER
(604) 737-0625 (ADMINISTRATION) OR (604) 739-0559 (BOX OFFICE)
WWW.FAXIMUM.COM/BARD

Now in its 11th season, the Bard on the Beach is a popular summertime festival featuring productions of three Shakespearean works performed under a large open tent by the beach. Few stages are as majestic with the cityscape and mountains as a backdrop.

There are matinee and evening shows. However, each performance is nearly three hours long and best suited for children over eight. If you do come with the family, bring a picnic and plan to arrive well before curtain time. Vanier

☞ **SEASONS AND TIMES**
➤ Mid-June—late Sept. Call the festival for a schedule of performances.

☞ **COST**
➤ Shows in June and Saturday matinees: $12.50 per person.
Other times: $23.50 per person.
Workshops: Call 737-0625.

☞ **GETTING THERE**

➤ By car, take Burrard St. south across the Burrard St. Bridge to Cornwall Ave. Turn north on Cypress St. (it's the second exit) and continue to the park. Limited free parking on site. About ten minutes from the Hotel Vancouver.

➤ By public transit, take city buses 2 or 22 south on Burrard to Cornwall and Cypress and walk north for a few minutes.

➤ By bike or on foot, take the Seaside Bicycle Route.

☞ **NEARBY**

➤ Vancouver Museum, City of Vancouver Archives, H.R. MacMillan Space Centre, Vancouver Maritime Museum, Southam Observatory, Kitsilano Beach Park, Seaside Bicycle Route.

Park has picnic tables and lots of room for kids to run around. Also bring cushions for the theatre's wooden seats, bug repellent and sweaters. It can get chilly by the water.

The Bard Company offers workshops to young thespians ages 8 to 18. During each two-week session company members will instruct the children in acting, voice, movement and other performance skills. After the course, they'll perform a play for their families and guests.

Sunny Days
THE VANCOUVER FOLK MUSIC FESTIVAL

JERICHO BEACH PARK
AT THE END OF POINT GREY RD.
VANCOUVER
(604) 602-9798
WWW.THEFESTIVAL.BC.CA

I f listening to music on the beach, snacking on delectables and taking a dip in the ocean all sound appealing, then head to Jericho Beach

Park during the Vancouver Folk Music Festival. The celebration runs for two days and three nights and features an international lineup of musicians who perform every style of folk music, from traditional and contemporary to folk fusion. The venue has seven stages, including one for children.

The festival offers more than music. Browsing at the market for clothing, musical instruments, CDs, books and delicious edible treats is fun too. Or head to the Little Folks section that features fun activities for kids, including instruction in Chinese calligraphy and origami. There's also face painting, a spray park and a play area with bean bags, tunnels and jumping balls.

If the forecast calls for hot, sunny weather, pack plenty of liquids and bring sunscreen, hats, a blanket and a beach umbrella. The festival site is large, so you might also want to bring a stroller for your toddler.

☞ **SEASONS AND TIMES**
➝ Usually the third weekend in July. Call 602-9798 for a schedule of events or visit the festival's Web site.

☞ **COST**
➝ Friday: Adults $35, youths (13 to 18) $22.
Saturday or Sunday: Adults $50, youths (13 to 18) $25.
Little Folks Area: Children (3 to 12) $6.
Weekend packages are available.
Tickets are available at all Ticketmaster outlets: www.ticketmaster.com

☞ **GETTING THERE**
➝ By car, take Burrard St. south across the Burrard St. Bridge to Cornwall Ave. and head west (Cornwall merges with Point Grey Rd.) to Jericho Park. Pay parking on site. About 25 minutes from the Hotel Vancouver.
➝ By public transit, take city bus 4 south on Granville Mall to the park.
➝ By bike or on foot, take the Seaside Bicycle Route. Bicycle parking by the East Gate.

☞ **NEARBY**
➝ Old Hastings Mill Museum, Pacific Spirit Park, University of British Columbia.

☞ **COMMENT**
➝ Plan at least a half-day visit.

Meet Me at the Fair
THE PACIFIC NATIONAL EXHIBITION

PACIFIC NATIONAL EXHIBITION GROUNDS
HASTINGS ST. AND RENFREW ST.
VANCOUVER
(604) 253-2311
WWW.PNE.BC.CA

The Pacific National Exhibition (PNE) promises families freewheeling fun and lots of excitement over 17 days. Kids of all ages will enjoy the midway rides and games of chance at Playland (page 96) For a taste of rural British Columbia, visit the fair's agriculture exhibitions with livestock shows and displays of farm produce. There is a petting zoo and kids can cuddle up to rabbits, goats, sheep and other friendly critters. When hunger strikes and you need a snack or a meal, you'll find dozens of food stands on the grounds.

Afterward, take in one of the PNE's daily spectacles. Music shows, dance performances and family favourites such as the RCMP Musical Ride and

☞ **SEASONS AND TIMES**
➤ Third weekend in August to the first weekend in September, daily, 10:30 am—midnight.

☞ **COST**
➤ General Admission: Adults $6, seniors and youths (6 to 18) $4, children (5 and under) free when accompanied by an adult.
General Ride Passport: $24.95.
Limited Ride Passport (under 122 cm): $21.95.
Techni-Cal Superdogs show extra.
Group rates available.

☞ **GETTING THERE**
➤ By car, take Burrard St. south to W. Hastings St. and go east (it becomes E. Hastings) to Renfrew St. The PNE is on the northeast corner. Pay parking on site. Also, some residents will rent their parking spaces. About 15 minutes from the Hotel Vancouver.
➤ By public transit, take city buses 4, 10 or 16 northbound from Granville St. to the PNE.

the Techni-Cal Superdogs show are just a few of the events scheduled through-out the day. Other popular PNE attractions include the Youth and Kids Talent Competitions, the Pola-

☞ **NEARBY**
→ Vancouver Port.

☞ **COMMENT**
→ Stroller and wheelchair rentals at the information centres. Plan at least a 3-hour visit.

ris Water Celebration and Parade, and the Demo-lition Derby. For times and locations of these and other shows, pick up a daily schedule when you enter the grounds.

Other Favourite Festivals
Symphony of Fire

ENGLISH BAY
VANCOUVER
(604) 738-4304

I f you want to be front and centre for this popular international pyrotechnics competition, get a jump on the crowds by grabbing a blanket and head-ing to the beach at English Bay well before the 10:15 pm starting time. The festival, which is held over two Saturday and two Wednesday nights, lights up the evening skies. To add to the enjoyment, music accom-panies the show. Spectacular views of the 30-minute presentations can also be had from Vanier Park Beach, Kitsilano Beach, Jericho Beach, Point Grey and Stanley Park. English Bay and the entire West End is only open to local traffic during the Symphony of Fire and public transportation is re-routed.

☞ Late July and early August. For exact dates, call 738-4304.

☞ Free.

Vancouver International Comedy Festival

GRANVILLE ISLAND AND OTHER VENUES AROUND TOWN
(604) 683-0883
WWW.COMEDYFEST.COM

The headline acts are guaranteed to provoke smiles to belly laughs, but not every show at Vancouver's International Comedy Festival is for children. For a dose of family entertainment, head to Triangle Square or Market Courtyard on Granville Island, where street performers put on shows daily over the course of the festival. The lineup of internationally renowned jugglers, clowns, fire-eaters and other wacky entertainers will have every member of your family in hysterics.

☞ Festival dates: Beginning the third week in July for 10 days.
Granville Island street shows: Daily, on the hour from noon to 4 pm.

☞ Granville Island street shows: Free.
For ticket information and schedules for the festival's other shows, call the Comedy Festival Hotline at 683-0883 or visit its Web site.

☞ Take Granville St. south across the Granville St. Bridge, then turn west on 4th Ave. and follow the signs.
Take city bus 50 south to Granville Island or take buses 8 or 10 and transfer to the 51 at Broadway. Or ride the Aquabus from the Aquatic Centre on Beach Ave.
➤ By bicycle or on foot, use the Seaside Bicycle Route to access Granville Island.

Canada Day

999 CANADA PLACE
VANCOUVER
(604) 666-5784

At 10:30 am on July 1st, tens of thousands of people gather at Canada Place to celebrate Canada's birthday. The day is brimming with all kinds of activities for

kids and families and there's plenty of live entertainment too. In fact, there's so much to see, some family
members might want to go exploring by themselves. If
that's the case, then arrange a place and a time where
you can meet afterward. And hold your younger children's hands, as there are crowds. Don't miss the
spectacular fireworks display that caps off the celebrations. Communities throughout the Lower Mainland
hold their own Canada Day parties and there are scheduled activities at Grouse Mountain and on Granville
Island. Check the local newspaper for details.

☞ July 1, 10:30 am—10:30 pm.

☞ Free.

☞ Follow Burrard St. north to the very foot of Burrard St.
Minutes from the Hotel Vancouver.

Harmony Arts Festival
JOHN LAWSON PARK AND ARGYLE AVE. (BETWEEN 13TH ST. AND 16TH ST.)
WEST VANCOUVER
(604) 925-7268

T he Harmony Arts Festival is a ten-day smorgas-
bord of visual arts exhibits, street craft fairs and
outdoor evening concerts featuring music from blues
to jazz. Devoted to giving North and West Vancouver
artists a venue for their works, the festival also offers
visitors displays of fabrics and textiles and hands-on
demonstrations in wood carving and seaweed basket
making. The festival has art and sculpture activities
for children and there's a week-long workshop called
"Kidding Around." Creative Kids Day offers face
painting, storytelling, mask making and drumming,
and there are performances by entertainers throughout the day. For more information on activities and

events, check the local paper, *North Shore News*, one week prior to the festival.

☞ Starts the first weekend in August and runs for ten days.

☞ Evening concerts and Creative Kids Day: Free.
There are fees for the week-long day camps and interactive digital animation workshops.

☞ Take Georgia St. west through Stanley Park across the Lions Gate Bridge. Take the West Vancouver Exit and continue along Marine Dr. past Park Royal Shopping Centre to 13th St. Park on the street.
Take the West Vancouver blue bus 250 on W. Georgia St.
By bike, follow the car directions.

Vancouver Storytelling Festival

VARIOUS VENUES AROUND VANCOUVER
(604) 876-2272
WWW.INTERNETSTORE.BC.CA/STORYTELLING

The Vancouver Storytelling Festival, which began in 1991, features a mix of local and international storytellers who regale audiences both young and old with their yarns. Choose to listen to a one-man show with many intertwined tales, or several storytellers reciting a story or two. There are daytime and evening shows and special shows for kids. Workshops are also offered. The times and locations for the performances vary each year, so call the festival for a schedule, or check the entertainment section of the local paper during the week of the festival. You'll also find information posted at Vancouver-area libraries.

☞ First or second week in November, daily.

☞ Afternoon shows $6, evening shows $12. Workshops $25. Special rates for children.

CHAPTER 12

FARTHER AFIELD

Introduction

While this guide was designed to provide you with a variety of fun outings within an hour of Vancouver, a few sites that are a bit farther afield couldn't be left out. You can take the family to explore an old-time general store and farm at Harrison Mills, or enjoy a weekend of waterslides and camping at Cultus Lake Provincial Park. Kids can never get enough of exotic animals, and they'll see plenty of them at the Greater Vancouver Zoo. If nosing about vintage aircraft is more your thing, head to the Canadian Museum of Flight in Langley. Other out-of-town destinations include Bowen Island and the resort at Whistler. While all these sites fall outside of the guide's "one-hour rule" for travel, after exploring them, you'll agree that they're well worth the extra drive.

The Five and Dime
KILBY HISTORIC STORE AND FARM

HARRISON MILLS
(604) 796-9576
WWW.ELP.GOV.BC.CA/BCPARKS/EXPLORE/PARKPGS/KILBY.HTM

Back in the Roaring '20s, Harrison Mills was a thriving mill town with a school, railway station, churches, homes, and of course the general store. Today, this picturesque town with its curious elevated walkways (Harrison Mills is on the Fraser River floodplain) is a quiet place—unless you visit Kilby Historic Store and Farm. Staff in period costume will guide you back to that time when shopping not only meant buying supplies, but also catching up on the local gossip, chatting with the storekeeper and picking up the mail.

The store houses several exhibits from the era, and you'll get to see the post office and the Kilby's living quarters. Afterward, head outside and explore the farm with its milk house and displays of equipment and cuddly animals that kids can visit. You can try

☞ **SEASONS AND TIMES**
➤ May–Oct, daily, 10 am–5 pm.

☞ **COST**
➤ Adults $6, children (6 to 14) $3, under 6 free, families $16.
Discounts for tour groups available.

☞ **GETTING THERE**
➤ By car, take Seymour St. north to Cordova St. (it eventually merges into Dundas) and go east to Nanaimo St. Take Nanaimo north to McGill St. and head east until the access to Hwy. 1 (Trans-Canada Hwy.) Take Hwy. 1 east to the Agassiz turnoff, turn north on Hwy. 9 and drive through Agassiz. Then head west for a few kilometres on Hwy. 7 to Harrison Mills. Free parking on site. About two hours from the Hotel Vancouver.

☞ **NEARBY**
➤ Dinotown, Harrison Lake and Hot Springs, Kilby Provincial Park, Harrison Mills, Weaver Creek Spawning Channel, Sasquatch Provincial Park.

☞ **COMMENT**
➤ Plan a 2-hour visit.

☞ **SIMILAR ATTRACTION**
➤ **Clayburn Village Store and Tea Shop.** Hundreds of jars of old-fashioned English sweets. 34810 Clayburn Rd., Abbotsford (604) 853-4020.

your hand (or foot) at walking on stilts and there's a horseshoe pitch, too. Feeling peckish? Steer your brood to the Harrison River Tea Room, which offers sit-down home-style cooking and take-out.

Don't miss Kilby's seasonal events when there's apple cider and ice-cream making, haunted house tours at Halloween and Railway Days. Call for a schedule of events. Guided tours for school groups (ages 6 to 15) are offered.

Three-point Landing
CANADIAN MUSEUM OF FLIGHT

HANGAR 2, LANGLEY AIRPORT
5333 - 216TH ST.
LANGLEY
(604) 532-0035
WWW.CANADIANFLIGHT.ORG

The Canadian Museum of Flight is the perfect place for the family to ogle gleaming vintage aircraft. The museum has 23 fully restored aircraft on display, including military jets, civilian aircraft, gliders and helicopters.

You can guide yourself inside the hanger, getting up-close views and touching classics such as a 1931 deHavilland DH82C Tiger Moth and a Waco AQC-6, a popular four-seat cabin biplane from the late 1930s. Two computers will show kids all the parts of an airplane and what makes it fly. There's also a wind tunnel demonstrating how an aircraft's wings react to high-speed winds.

In the courtyard outside, you'll find a unique collection of restored antique Canadian aircraft, including a 1942 Handley Page Hampden from the Second World War and a Canadair CF-104 Starfighter. Don't forget to stop in at the Douglas DC3 compound where kids can climb aboard the air-

☞ **SEASONS AND TIMES**
→ Year-round: Daily, 10 am—4 pm.

☞ **COST**
→ Adults $5, seniors and students $4, children under 6 free, families (two adults and two children) $12.

☞ **GETTING THERE**
→ By car, take Seymour St. north to Cordova St. (it eventually merges into Dundas) and go east to Nanaimo St. Take Nanaimo north to McGill St. and head east until the access to Hwy. 1 (Trans-Canada Hwy.) Follow Hwy. 1 east to Langley, get off at the 200th St. Exit and drive south towards Langley. Turn east onto the Langley Bypass and continue until 56th Ave. Turn east on 56th, drive to 216th St. and then turn south. Turn west immediately after you pass the DC-3 Terminal. Free parking on site. About one hour from the Hotel Vancouver.

☞ **NEARBY**
→ Langley Centennial Museum, Fort Langley, Campbell Valley Regional Park, Greater Vancouver Zoo.

☞ **COMMENT**
→ Plan a 1-hour visit.

plane and examine the cockpit. Guided tours are available (groups of ten or more) with reservations.

Day Tripping on
BOWEN ISLAND

(604) 947-9024
WWW.BOWENISLAND.COM

For a day that's filled with fun activities outdoors, hop aboard the *Queen of Capilano* ferry at Horseshoe Bay and ride it to Bowen Island. Home to 3,000 year-round residents, the island also offers endless pleasures to visitors who come for the day. When you dock at Snug Cove, make your way to the Union Steamship Company General Store where a tourist information centre has maps to show you all of the area's attractions.

Crippen Regional Park is minutes away from Snug Cove and features a variety of hiking trails, pretty footbridges, boardwalks, a lagoon and Killarney Lake, which is warm enough for summer swimming. Keep your eyes peeled for ducks, kingfishers, swallows and herons, which frequent the park's rich marshlands. In the park you'll find plenty of picnic areas with scenic views, or return to Snug Cove for fish and chips at

☞ **SEASONS AND TIMES**

→ Park: Year-round, dawn—dusk. The ferry makes several crossings each day between 7 am and 9:45 pm. Call 1-888-223-3779 for the exact times.

☞ **COST**

→ Park: Free. Ferry: Adults $5.75, children (5 to 11) $3, under 5 free. Bicycles $1.50.

☞ **GETTING THERE**

→ By car, take Georgia St. west across the Lions Gate Bridge and take the West Vancouver Exit. Turn north at the first set of lights (Park Royal Mall and Taylor Way) and follow the signs to Hwy. 1 W. Continue on and follow the signs to the ferry terminal at Horseshoe Bay. Pay parking on site. About two hours from the Hotel Vancouver.

→ By public transit, take the West Vancouver Municipal Transit (Blue Bus) Express bus 257 on the corner of Georgia St. and Granville St. and ride it to the ferry terminal.

a local eatery. If it's a warm day, bring swimsuits for everyone and head to Deep Bay for a refreshing dip. Bike and kayak rentals are available. For bike rentals, call (604) 947-0707. For kayak rentals, call (604) 947-0266.

> ☞ **SIMILAR ATTRACTION**
> ➤ **Barnston Island.** Ride the ferry to Barnston Island and then bike the 9.8 kilometre circuit. There are plenty of sandy beaches that are perfect for having a picnic. Call Greater Vancouver Regional District at (604) 432-6350.

Hanging Out at CULTUS LAKE PROVINCIAL PARK

COLUMBIA VALLEY PKWY.
CHILLIWACK
1-604-858-8121 OR 1-800-567-9535
WWW.TOURISMCHILLIWACK.COM
WWW.ENV.GOV.BC.CA/BCPARKS/EXPLORE/PARKPGS/CULTUS.HTM

A haven for families, Cultus Lake Provincial Park is a fabulous place for a weekend getaway, or day trip out of the city. Start your excursion off right by hiking along one of the park's trails, such as the Teapot Hill Trail, a five-kilometre stroll that takes you past Cultus Lake and the Columbia Valley. At Cultus Lake, there are two boat rental shops, great swimming beaches, a quaint little village with a few shops, riding stables

> ☞ **SEASONS AND TIMES**
> ➤ Park: Year-round, 8 am—dusk. Only registered campers allowed between 10:30 pm and 8 am.
>
> ☞ **COST**
> ➤ Park: Free.
> Camping: Call 1-800-698-9025 or visit www.discovercamping.ca for details.

☞ **GETTING THERE**

➤ By car, take Seymour St. north to Cordova St. (it eventually merges into Dundas) and go east to Nanaimo St. Take Nanaimo north to McGill St. and head east to access Hwy. 1 (Trans-Canada Hwy.) Take Hwy. 1 east to Exit 104 and continue going east through Yarrow to Cultus Lake. Free parking on site. About 90 minutes from the Hotel Vancouver.

☞ **NEARBY**

➤ Bridal Veil Falls, Sasquatch Provincial Park, Kilby Historic Store and Farm, Eagle Ridge Adventure Golf, Dinotown, Minter Gardens,

☞ **COMMENT**

➤ Plan to visit for the day, or several days.

☞ **SIMILAR ATTRACTION**

➤ **Trans-Canada Water Slides**, Bridal Falls Rd. (intersection of Hwy. 1 and Hwy. 9), Chilliwack (604) 794-7455.

and a barnyard filled with friendly animals. The park also boasts two golf and two minigolf courses, bumper boats, go-carts and canoe and jet-ski rentals.

If you are looking for something more adventurous, sign up for white water rafting down the Chilliwack River. Or, head across the lake to Cultus Lake Waterpark (604-858-7241), where your kids can splish splash the day away riding daredevil slides or playing in the wavepools.

With so much to do, there's little doubt you'll want to hang out in this neck of the woods a little longer. So, pack the camping gear and spend a night or two under the stars at one of the park's four campgrounds.

Aardvarks to Zebras at the
GREATER VANCOUVER ZOO

5048 - 264TH ST.
ALDERGROVE
(604) 857-9005
WWW.GREATERVANCOUVERZOO.COM

Whether you choose to wheel, in-line skate, cycle, walk or push a stroller through the Greater Vancouver Zoo, you'll be in for a real treat. The zoo has over 200 species on display including giraffe, zebra, rhinos, tigers, bears and wolves, just to name a few. Most of the animals roam freely in large pens amidst authentic recreations of their natural habitat. Pop in to the Vivarium where the zoo's collection of reptiles and amphibians is housed.

If you have little ones in tow, take them for a tour of the grounds aboard the Safari Express Train or the Happy Hippo Bus. Be sure to leave time for the petting zoo, where Anthony the pot-bellied pig will squeal a greeting when you step inside.

The zoo has birthday packages and there are Sleep on the Wild Side

☞ **SEASONS AND TIMES**
➤ Year-round: Daily, 9 am—dusk.

☞ **COST**
➤ Adults (16 to 64) $10.50, seniors (65 and up) and children (3 to 15) $7.50, under 2 free.
Group rates and annual memberships are available, call 856-6825. Miniature train tours and the Hippo Bus: $2 per person.

☞ **GETTING THERE**
➤ By car, take Seymour St. north to Cordova St. (it eventually merges into Dundas) and go east to Nanaimo St. Take Nanaimo to McGill St. Drive east and access Hwy. 1 (Trans-Canada Hwy.) Take Hwy. 1 east to Langley. Take Exit 73 at 264th St. and head south and look for signs for the zoo. Pay parking on site. About one hour from the Hotel Vancouver.

☞ **NEARBY**
➤ Aldergrove Telephone Museum and Community Archives. Fort Langley Historical Site and Museum, Canadian Museum of Flight, Campbell Valley Regional Park.

☞ **COMMENT**
➤ There are machines with animal feed located throughout the zoo, bring plenty of change. Plan a 3 to 4-hour visit.

sleepovers. Educators take note: lesson plans, activities and studies ideas are available. The zoo's calendar of events includes daily animal demonstrations and feedings, as well as seasonal activities and evening programs. Call for details.

Powder Perfect
WHISTLER RESORT

4010 WHISTLER WAY
WHISTLER
(604) 932-3928

More than just a destination for skiers, Whistler Resort offers families a fantastic range of activities any time of the year. In summer, there's alpine hiking, canoeing, kayaking, golfing and fishing. Or how about taking the gang sailboarding, horseback riding or skateboarding? Mountain bikes can be rented from most of the outfitting shops in Whistler, and there are five lakes in the area with sandy swimming beaches, picnic facilities and green spaces. Don't miss Blackcomb's Adventure Zone, which has minigolf, a circus trapeze, a climbing wall and other activities.

If the weather turns foul, then explore Whistler indoors. The **Meadow Park Sports Centre** has a regulation-size arena offering year-round skating, squash courts and a wading pool just for kids. There's also a movie theatre, an arcade with high-tech games and a bowling alley. Family restaurants abound in Whistler, so you won't have to go far to find food your kids like.

Also a world-class alpine resort, Whistler and Blackcomb mountains offer some of the best downhill and telemarking skiing in North America. Both establishments also have halfpipes and large terrain parks for snowboarders. Lessons and equipment rentals are available for all ages and levels, so don't let anything hold you back.

Call 1-800 WHISTLER or 1-800-944-7853 for information on accommodations.

☞ **SEASONS AND TIMES**
➤ Year-round: Daily.

☞ **GETTING THERE**
➤ By car, follow Georgia St. west across the Lions Gate Bridge and take the turn-off for West Vancouver. Follow Marine Dr. W. to Taylor Way. Head north and access Hwy. 1 W. (Upper Levels Hwy.), which becomes Hwy. 99 N. (Sea to Sky). Stay on Hwy. 99 all the way to Whistler. Pay parking on site. About two hours from the Hotel Vancouver.
➤ By bus, Greyhound Canada (604-482-8747 or 1-800-661-8747) has a daily express bus to Whistler. Greyhound Bus Lines has a Vancouver to Whistler service with stops along the way (1-800-661-8747 www.greyhound.ca) By train, B.C. Rail (604-984-5246) operates a train to Whistler that departs daily at 7 am from the B.C. Rail Station in North Vancouver.
For information about public transit around Whistler, call (604) 932-4020.

☞ **COMMENT**
➤ Snow chains or good winter tires are advisable in the winter season. Plan to spend the day or longer.

12 Months of Fun!
DIRECTORY OF EVENTS

JANUARY

To early January
Heritage Christmas
Burnaby Village
(604) 293-6500

New Year's Day
Polar Bear Swim
English Bay
(604) 665-3424

Late January
Winterfest
Marpole Community Centre
(604) 879-8611

Late January to early February
Chinese New Year Festival and
Parade
Chinatown
(604) 682-8998

FEBRUARY

To early February
Chinese New Year Festival and
Parade
Chinatown
(604) 682-8998

Early February
Vancouver Boat Show
B.C. Place Stadium
(604) 294-1313

Mid-February
B.C. Adventure Sports Show
B.C. Place Stadium
(905) 477-2677

Late February
West Vancouver Heritage Week
(604) 925-7236 or (604) 925-7295

MARCH

Late March to early April
Pacific International Auto and
Light Truck Show
B.C. Place Stadium
(604) 214-9964

APRIL

Mid-April
Vancouver Sun Fun Run
(604) 689-9441

Mid-April
Bradner Daffodil Festival
Community Hall, Bradner
(604) 856-2794

MAY

Early May
Vancouver International
Marathon
(604) 872-2928

Early May
Opening Day
West Coast Railway Heritage
Park, Squamish
1-800-722-1233

Early May
Annual Burnaby Rhododendron
Festival
Deer Lake, Burnaby
(604) 291-6864

Mid-May
Pacific Spirit Run
Pacific Spirit Park
(604) 877-3340

Mid-May
Bluegrass Festival
Granville Island
(604) 666-5784

Mid-May
CityFest
Vancouver City College
(604) 871-7000

Mid-May to mid-June
Whistler Summer Street
Entertainment
Whistler
(604) 932-2394

Late-May
Vancouver International
Children's Festival
Vanier Park
(604) 708-5655

Late May
Hyack Festival
New Westminster
(604) 522-6894

Late May
Cloverdale Rodeo
Cloverdale Fairgrounds, Surrey
(604) 576-9461

JUNE
Early June
Teddy Bear Picnic and Parade
Town Centre Stadium
(604) 473-1615

Early June
Slugfest
Richmond Nature Park
(604) 273-7015

Early June
Ethnic Day
Queensborough Community
Centre, New Westminster
(604) 525-7388

Mid-June to late September
Bard on the Beach Shakespeare
Festival
Vanier Park
(604) 737-0625 or (604) 739-
0559 (box office)

To mid-June
Whistler Summer Street
Entertainment
Whistler
(604) 932-2394

Mid-June
Alcan International Dragon Boat
Festival
False Creek and Plaza of Nations
(604) 688-2382

Mid-June
Aboriginal Art & Culture
Celebration
Robson Square Conference
Centre
(604) 280-4444 (tickets) or
(604) 683-2000 (information)

Mid-June
Kitsilano Soap Box Derby
(604) 731-4454

Mid-June
Francophone Summer Festival
(festival d'été)
Various venues around town.
(604) 736-9806

Late June
Point Grey Fiesta Days
and Parade
(604) 257-8140

Late June to early July
Du Maurier International
Jazz Festival
Various venues around town.
(604) 872-5200

Late June to early July
Fort Langley Festival of the
Performing Arts
Fort Langley
(604) 888-1759

Late June to August
Kitsilano Showboat
(604) 734-7332

JULY
To early July
Du Maurier International Jazz
Festival
Various venues around town.
(604) 872-5200

To early July
Fort Langley Festival of the
Performing Arts
(604) 888-1759

Bard on the Beach Shakespeare
Festival
Vanier Park
(604) 737-0625
or (604) 739-0559 (box office)

Kitsilano Showboat
(604) 734-7332

Canada Day Festivities
Canada Place and various venues
across the Lower Mainland.
(604) 666-7200 or 666-8477

Early July
Festa Italian
Italian Centre
(604) 430-3377

Early July
Salmon Festival
Steveston
(604) 718-8080

Early July to mid-July
Dancing on the Edge Festival
(10 day festival)
Firehall Arts Centre
(604) 689-0926

Mid-July
North Fraser Harbour Days
Various locations along the
North Arm of the Fraser River.
(604) 273-1866

Mid-July
Vancouver Folk Music Festival
Jericho Beach Park
(604) 602-9798

Mid-July to mid-August
Theatre Under the Stars
Malkin Bowl
(604) 687-0174

Mid-July to mid-August
Early Music Festival Concert
series
UBC Recital Hall
(604) 732-1610

Late July
Discovery Days
Burnaby Lake, Burnaby
(604) 291-6864

Late July
Night of 2000 Lights
Various venues in the Greater
Vancouver area.
(604) 879-8611

Late July
International Bog Day
Burns Bog Conservation Society
(604) 572-0373

Late July
Vancouver International
Comedy Festival
Various venues around town.
(604) 683-0883

Late July
Caribbean Days Festival
Waterfront Park
(604) 515-2400
or (604) 987-7529

Late July
Whistler Country and Blues
Festival
Whistler
(604) 664-5625

Late July
Whistler Roots Festival
Whistler Village
(604) 664-5625

Late July to early August
Benson and Hedges Symphony
of Fire
English Bay
(604) 738-4304

Late July to mid-August
Vancouver Chamber Music
Festival
Vanier Park and Crofton House
School
(604) 602-0363

August
To early August
Benson and Hedges Symphony
of Fire
English Bay
(604) 738-4304

Bard on the Beach Shakespeare
Festival
Vanier Park
(604) 737-0625
or (604) 739-0559 (box office)

Early August
Powell Street Festival
Oppenheimer Park
(604) 739-9388

Early August
Abbotsford International
Airshow
Abbotsford
(604) 852-8511

Early August
Harmony Arts Festival
West Vancouver
(604) 925-7268

To mid-August
Vancouver Chamber Music
Festival
Vanier Park and Crofton House
School
(604) 602-0363

To late August
Kitsilano Showboat
(604) 734-7332

Late August
Vancouver Wooden Boat Show
Granville Island
Displays and Hands-on Boat
Building
(604) 519-7400

Late August to early September
Pacific National Exhibition
(PNE)
Exhibition Park
(604) 253-2311

September
To early September
Pacific National Exhibition
(PNE)
Exhibition Park
(604) 253-2311

Labour Day weekend
Molson Indy Vancouver
False Creek
(604) 684-4639

Terry Fox Run
(604) 464-2666

**Early September to mid-
September**
Vancouver Fringe Festival
Various venues around town.
(604) 257-0350

Early to mid-September
Whistler Jazz & Blue Weekend
Whistler Resort
(604) 932-3938

To late September
Bard on the Beach Shakespeare
Festival
Vanier Park
(604) 737-0625
or (604) 739-0559 (box office)

Late September to early October
Vancouver International Film
Festival
Various venues around town.
(604) 685-0260

OCTOBER
To early October
Vancouver International Film
Festival
Various venues around town.

Early October
Cranberry Harvest Festival
Richmond Nature Park
(604) 273-7015

Early to late October
Celebrate the Arts
26 cultural events at various
venues around town.
(604) 685-7811

Late October
Vancouver International Writers
(& Readers) Festival
Granville Island
(604) 681-6330

NOVEMBER
Snow Goose Month
(see migrating snow geese)
Reifel Bird Sanctuary
Ladner
(604) 946-6980

Early November
Parents and Kids Show
Vancouver Trade and
Convention Centre
1-877-822-8599

Early November
Vancouver Storytelling Festival
Various locations around town.
(604) 876-2272

Early November
Hadassah Bazaar
Pacific National Exhibition
(604) 257-5160

Early November to mid-November
Circle Craft Christmas Market
Trade & Convention Centre
(604) 669-8021

Mid-November
Hycroft Christmas
Hycroft Manor
(604) 731-4661

DECEMBER
Early December to late December
Christmas Under the Sails
Canada Place
(604) 666-8477

December to early January
Heritage Christmas
Burnaby Village
(604) 293-6500

Early December
Santa Claus Parade
Columbia St., New Westminster
(604) 524-6894

Early December to mid-December
Christmas Carol Ship Festival
and Parade
Various parks in the Greater
Vancouver area.
(604) 926-7290

**Early December
to late December**
Festival of Lights
VanDusen Gardens
(604) 878-9274

**Mid-December
to late December**
Christmas at Canada Place
Canada Place
(604) 666-8477

Late December
Winter Solstice Lantern
Procession
False Creek Community Centre
(604) 257-8195

INDEX

Notes

Notes

Notes